Management of

Ocular
Emergencies

3rd Edition

Raymond Stein, MD, FRCSC
Harold Stein, MD, FRCSC

 Medicöpea

National Library of Canada Cataloguing in Publication Data

Main entry under title:
Management of ocular emergencies
3rd ed.
ISBN 1-896825-12-5

Previous eds published as: Management of ocular emergencies / Raymond Stein, Harold Stein, Bernard Slatt.

1. Ophthalmologic emergencies. I. Stein, Raymond M. II. Stein, Harold A. Management of ocular emergencies.

RE48.9.S83 2002   617.7'1   C2001-904026-1

Applications and usage

The authors and publisher have exerted every effort to ensure that the applications and use of all drugs, devices, and procedures mentioned in this publication are in accord with current recommendations and practices. However, in view of ongoing research, changes in regulations, and the constant flow of information relating to ophthalmology, the reader is cautioned to consult the package insert of any product for the approved indications and dosage recommendations in Canada as well as for the incidence of adverse reactions and mortality.

This book has been made possible by an unrestricted medical education grant from Alcon Canada.

Prepared, printed, and published in Montreal, Canada, by:

Medicöpea International Inc.
3333 Cote Vertu Blvd., Suite 300
Montreal, Quebec
H4R 2N1 Canada
ISBN: 1-896825-12-5

Copyright 2002 Medicöpea International Inc.

Contents

Introduction

This manual is designed to be a practical guide to the management of ocular emergencies, and presents the clinical principles used in our everyday ophthalmic practice. The material arose from a series of lectures given to emergency room physicians, medical students, and ophthalmology residents, and was enthusiastically received for its simplified approach and organization.

An attempt has been made to organize the material into clinically relevant sections. The first section highlights the essentials of the eye examination. The next section deals with the emergency ocular diseases, and is divided into those diseases in which the patient presents with either a red eye or a white eye. The red eye conditions are those that may be nontraumatic or secondary to trauma; the white eye conditions are those that are associated with a decrease in vision or diplopia. The final section contains a series of appendixes that may be helpful for the differential diagnosis of a variety of emergency cases.

This third edition has been completely updated which is a reflection of the medical advances in diagnostic techniques and therapeutics. In addition, the color plates have been expanded in number and highlight the ocular conditions described in the text.

We hope that this manual will serve as a useful guide to the clinician for the management of ocular emergencies.

Raymond M. Stein, MD, FRCSC
Harold A. Stein, MD, FRCSC

Ocular History and Examination

Introduction

The type and characteristics of the presenting symptoms can often suggest a provisional diagnosis prior to the examination. The nature of the symptoms should be recorded, including any precipitating factors, whether the episode is recurrent, constant, or intermittent, and whether the onset was gradual or acute. Common symptoms include decreased vision, redness, photophobia, tearing, itching, foreign body sensation, burning, pain, diplopia, and floaters.

A brief medical history should be obtained. A variety of systemic diseases can affect the eye, including diabetes mellitus, hypertension, thyroid disease, rheumatoid arthritis, and cancer (Appendixes A,B). All medications should be documented, as certain systemic medications can cause ocular complications (Appendix C). Drug allergies should be determined before eye drops are instilled or medications prescribed. Any family history of ocular diseases should be recorded.

An examination should then be conducted, and will usually include a test of visual acuity, pupils, motility, confrontation visual field, the anterior segment, the posterior segment, and intraocular pressure (Figs. 1-3, Plate 1).

Visual Acuity

Check the distance visual acuity (VA) for each eye. Vision measurement is crucial for proper diagnosis, management, and medical/legal documentation. If a patient is

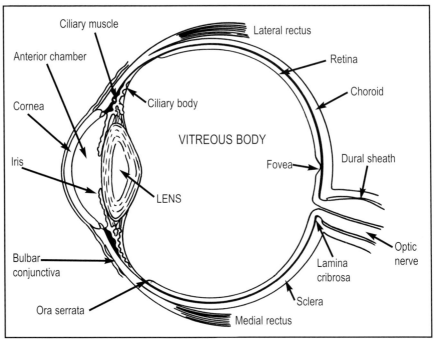

Fig. 1 The eye cut in longitudinal section

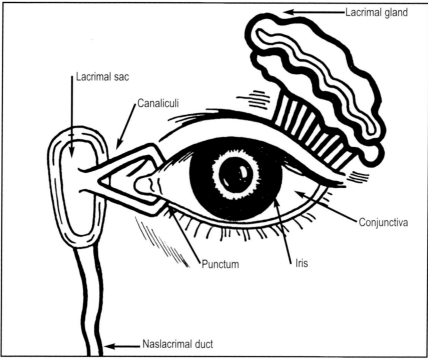

Fig. 2 Lacrimal apparatus. Tears produced by the lacrimal gland are drained through the punctum, lacrimal sac, and nasolacrimal duct into the nose.

unable to open his or her eye because of pain, a drop of topical anesthetic will usually reduce the pain enough to obtain a visual acuity.

Distance VA is usually checked at 20 feet (6 meters) using letters, numbers, or an illiterate E chart. In order of best to worst vision, acuities recorded are as follows: 20/15, 20/20, 20/25, 20/30, 20/40, 20/50, 20/60, 20/70, 20/80, 20/100, 20/200, 20/400, counting fingers, hand movements, light perception, and no light perception. The patient may view the visual acuity chart with both eyes either intentionally or unintentionally, if the examiner does not take care to see that one eye is completely occluded. If a patient has a VA of 20/60, this means that he sees at 20 feet what a person sees at 60 feet. Similarly, a VA of 20/15 means that he sees at 20 feet what a person sees at 15 feet. A patient will often read additional smaller letters on the chart with encouragement by the examiner, thereby increasing the accuracy of the examination data. For preschool-aged children, the "illiterate E" chart is used by having the child indicate the direction in which the legs of the "E" are pointing. Near vision is usually checked with a reading card held at 14 inches. This is the most convenient way to check vision in the hospitalized patient. The following are common abbreviations used to discuss visual acuity: OD (oculus dexter): right eye; OS (oculus sinister): left eye; OU (uterque): both eyes.

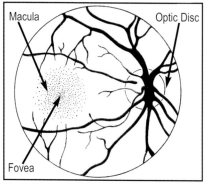

Fig. 3 Fundus diagram

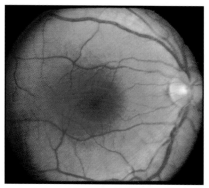

Plate 1 Normal fundus which shows the optic disc, blood vessels, macula, and fovea

If the patient has corrective lenses, they should be worn during testing. The examiner must try to determine optimum acuity. If the vision is less than 20/20, the potential for improved vision should be ascertained by having the patient look through a pinhole. Improved vision with a pinhole indicates that appropriate glasses or contact lenses would be beneficial; unimproved vision suggests that a non-refractive problem such as corneal edema, cataracts, or macular degeneration may exist. Visual acuity should be checked in both eyes since some patients are unaware of an amblyopic eye. If the good eye of such a patient is patched, he may be at serious risk of a motor vehicle accident when he drives.

In estimating visual acuity in the uncooperative patient, withdrawal or a change in facial expression in response to light or sudden movement indicates the presence of vision. A brisk pupillary response to light also suggests the presence of vision. The exception to this is the patient with cortical blindness, which is due to bilateral widespread destruction of the visual cortex. If there is any doubt, referral to an ophthalmologist is recommended.

Normal acuity does not ensure that significant vision has not been lost, since the entire visual field including peripheral vision must be considered. For instance, a patient who has lost all of the peripheral vision to one side — homonymous hemianopia — generally has normal visual acuity.

Pupils

The pupillary size and reaction to light stimulation should be checked, carefully noting the presence of a dilated or constricted pupil. The swinging flashlight test is used to determine the absence or presence of an afferent pupillary defect. It should be tested in all cases of decreased vision and head or eye trauma. Pupillary shape gives an indication of an eye's response to trauma. Eccentricity of pupillary shape after trauma can indicate serious ocular damage. A peaked or teardrop-shaped pupil may indicate a ruptured globe.

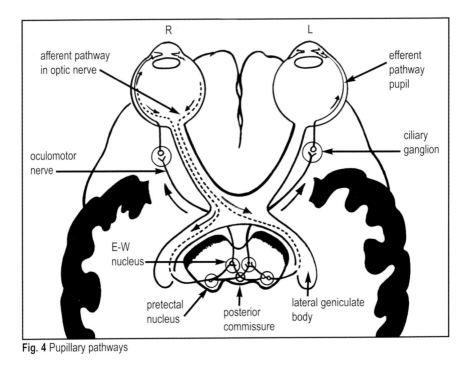

Fig. 4 Pupillary pathways

Figure 4 shows a cross section of the pupillary pathways. The solid line represents the efferent pathway and the broken line represents the afferent pathway. Light stimulation of the left retina will result in impulses which travel up the left optic nerve and divide at the chiasm. Some impulses continue up to the left tract; some crossing continues up to the right tract. The nerve impulses arrive at each pretectal nucleus and stimulate cells which in turn send impulses down the third cranial nerve to the iris sphincter causing each pupil to constrict. It is because of the double decussation, the first in the chiasm and the second between the pretectal nuclei and the Edinger-Westphal nuclei, that the direct pupil response in the left eye equals the consensual response in the right eye.

Swinging Flashlight Test

During the swinging flashlight test the examiner projects the light on the right eye (for example), allowing the right pupil to constrict to a minimum size and subsequently escape to an intermediate size. The light is then quickly swung to the left eye, which constricts from an intermediate to a minimum size, subsequently escaping to an intermediate size. At this point the light is swung again to the right eye and a mental note is made of the intermediate (starting) pupil size and briskness of the response to light. These characteristics should be exactly the same in both eyes as the light is alternately swung to each eye.

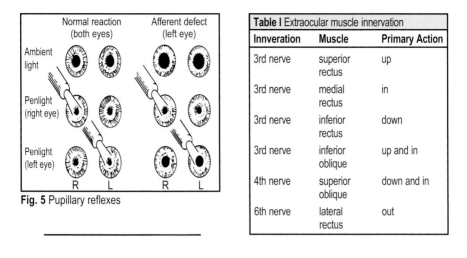

Fig. 5 Pupillary reflexes

The figure shows pupillary reflexes with columns for Normal reaction (both eyes) and Afferent defect (left eye), and rows for Ambient light, Penlight (right eye), and Penlight (left eye), labeled R and L.

Table I Extraocular muscle innervation		
Innervation	Muscle	Primary Action
3rd nerve	superior rectus	up
3rd nerve	medial rectus	in
3rd nerve	inferior rectus	down
3rd nerve	inferior oblique	up and in
4th nerve	superior oblique	down and in
6th nerve	lateral rectus	out

Afferent Pupillary Defect (Marcus-Gunn Pupil)

The swinging flashlight test will determine if the amount of light transmitted from one eye is less than that carried via the fellow eye; when the light is swung to the defective eye, immediate dilatation of the pupil occurs instead of the normal initial constriction. This characterizes an afferent pupillary defect (Fig. 5). The differential diagnosis includes a retinal detachment, occlusion of a central retinal artery or vein, optic neuritis, and optic neuropathy.

N.B.: Cataract, hyphema, vitreous hemorrhage, corneal ulcer, and iritis are associated with a decrease in vision, but are *not associated with an afferent pupillary defect*.

Differential Diagnosis of a Dilated Pupil

A dilated pupil may be due to third nerve palsy, trauma, Adie's pupil, acute glaucoma, or may be drug-induced.

Third Nerve Palsy. If the dilated pupil is fixed, the cause may be third nerve palsy. This condition may be associated with ptosis and a motility disturbance, characterized by the eye being deviated out and down. The pupil responds to constricting drops, e.g., pilocarpine. This is a neurosurgical emergency, as the possibility of an intracranial mass lesion must be ruled out.

Trauma. Damage to the iris sphincter may result from a blunt or penetrating injury. Iris transillumination defects may be visible with the ophthalmoscope or slit lamp, and the pupil may have an irregular shape.

Adie's Pupil. The pupil responds better to near stimulation than to light. The condition is thought to be related to aberrant innervation of the iris by axons which normally stimulate the ciliary body.

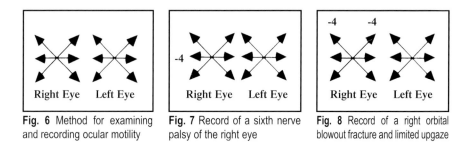

Fig. 6 Method for examining and recording ocular motility

Fig. 7 Record of a sixth nerve palsy of the right eye

Fig. 8 Record of a right orbital blowout fracture and limited upgaze

---

Drug-Induced. Iatrogenic or self-contamination may occur with a variety of dilating drops, e.g., cyclopentolate hydrochloride (Cyclogyl®), tropicamide (Mydriacyl®), homatropine, scopolamine, and atropine. The pupil is fixed and dilated and, unlike in third nerve palsy, does not respond to constricting drops.

Acute Glaucoma. The patient may complain of pain and/or nausea and vomiting. The eye is red, the vision is diminished, the intraocular pressure is elevated, and the pupil is mid-dilated and poorly reactive.

Differential Diagnosis of a Constricted Pupil
A constricted pupil occurs in Horner's syndrome, iritis, and may be drug-induced.

Horner's Syndrome. Other signs of this condition include mild ptosis of the upper lid and retraction of the lower lid. The difference in pupillary size is more notable in dim light since adrenergic innervation to the iris dilator muscle is diminished.

Drug-Induced. Iatrogenic or self-induced pupillary constriction may be due to a variety of drugs, including pilocarpine, carbachol, and echothiophate iodide (Phospholine Iodide®).

Iritis. Slit-lamp examination shows keratic precipitates and cells in the anterior chamber, and there is a prominent ciliary flush. The intraocular inflammation stimulates pupillary constriction.

Motility
There are six extraocular muscles in each eye that are innervated by a total of three nerves. The action of a specific muscle can vary depending on the position of the eye when it is innervated. Table I shows the general relationships which apply. Trauma to the muscles and/or cranial nerves serving the muscles can result in asymmetric movement of the eyes resulting in double vision when both eyes are open.

The examiner should determine the range of ocular movements in all gaze positions (Fig. 6). Limited movement in any gaze position can be documented as –1 (minimal), –2 (moderate), –3 (severe), or –4 (total). For example, a patient with a complete right sixth nerve palsy can be recorded as shown in Figure 7. Figure 8 shows a patient with a blow-out fracture to the right orbit with entrapment of the inferior rectus muscle and limitation of upgaze.

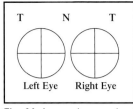

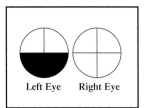

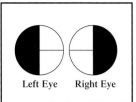

Fig. 9A A normal gross visual field test. T = temporal field; N = nasal field

Fig. 9B An inferior field defect of the left eye; the right is normal.

Fig. 9C A complete bitemporal visual field defect

Confrontation Visual Fields

A visual field defect may be caused by a disturbance of any of the neurologic pathways for light transmission. This includes the retina, optic disc, optic nerve, optic chiasm, optic tract, optic radiations, and occipital cortex.

A screening test for gross visual field loss can be performed as follows:

1. One eye of the patient is covered.
2. With the uncovered eye the patient must maintain fixation, e.g., on the tip of the examiner's nose.
3. The examiner randomly projects fingers in any quadrant, while standing 3 or 4 feet from the patient. For the detection of more subtle defects such as in optic neuritis, it is best to stand 10 to 20 feet away from the patient. The further one is from the patient, the greater the size of the scotoma.
4. The patient counts the projected fingers.

A normal response would be recorded as shown in Figure 9A. A patient with a retinal detachment of the superior retina would have an inferior field defect (Fig. 9B). A patient with a pituitary tumor may present initially with visual loss and a complete bitemporal defect (Fig. 9C). A more detailed evaluation of the visual field requires an automated machine. The target size and luminosity can be varied and the patient's response documented on a computer-generated printout.

Anterior Segment

Examination of the anterior segment should include an assessment of the lids, orbit, puncta, conjunctiva, sclera, cornea, anterior chamber, and lens (Fig. 10). In all suspected infectious cases, cotton swabs are used or gloves are worn to depress or elevate lids. This protects the examiner from contamination. Be careful not to put any pressure on the globe, especially in traumatic cases in which there is a possibility of an ocular perforation.

Examination of the orbit is important in trauma and in cases of periorbital swelling and erythema. In cases of trauma the orbital exam should include: 1. palpation for subcutaneous emphysema (air in subcutaneous tissues causing crepitus); 2. testing for localized areas of anesthesia (especially in the inferior orbit and cheek area); 3. palpation for defects in the orbital rim; 4. documenting the presence of proptosis or enophthalmos.

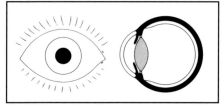

Fig. 10 Examination of the anterior segment includes an assessment of the lids, puncta, conjunctiva, sclera, cornea, anterior chamber, and lens

In a red eye, the conjunctiva should be examined to differentiate conjunctival hyperemia (blood vessel engorgement), subconjunctival hemorrhage (blood beneath the conjunctiva), a ciliary flush (injection of vessels around the cornea), or a combination of these. The examination should also check for the presence of conjunctival discharge, which, if detected, should be categorized as to its amount (profuse or scant) and character (muco-purulent or serous).

Pre-auricular lymph node enlargement is frequently a sign of viral conjunctivitis. Usually such enlargement does not occur in acute bacterial conjunctivitis.

In a patient who presents with a chronic conjunctivitis, one should rule out the possibility of a lacrimal system obstruction. Pressure on the lacrimal sac may produce the reflex of a mucous or purulent discharge from the puncta.

Fluorescein stain can be used to detect de-epithelialized surfaces, e.g., corneal abrasions, erosions, dendrites, and ulcers; epithelial defects stain green. Fluorescein is applied in the form of a sterile filter paper strip that is moistened with a drop of an artificial tear or saline solution and then touches the conjunctiva. A few blinks spread the fluorescein over the cornea. Viewing the eye under a cobalt blue light enhances the visibility of the green fluorescence. Fluorescein staining of the cornea should be assessed in all cases of "red eye" and trauma. Two precautions to keep in mind when using fluorescein are: 1. Use fluorescein-impregnated strips instead of stock solutions of fluorescein because such solutions are especially susceptible to contamination, with Pseudomonas species, and 2. Have the patient remove his or her contact lenses prior to application to avoid discoloration. Rose bengal stain also detects de-epithelialized surfaces, and in addition stains devitalized cells, as are found in the conjunctiva in keratitis sicca or chemical toxicity.

Superficial foreign bodies may be hidden under the inner surface of the upper lid or high in the cul-de-sac (formed by the junction of upper lid and conjunctiva of the globe). When a superficial keratitis occurs without evidence of a foreign body, the upper lid should be everted. To evert the upper lid the patient is asked to look downward and the examiner grasps the eyelashes of the upper lid between the thumb and the index finger. A cotton tip applicator may be used to press gently downward over the superior aspect of the tarsal plate as the lid margin is pulled upward by the lashes. Pressure is maintained on the everted upper lid while the patient is encouraged to keep looking downward. To return the lid to its normal position, the examiner releases the lid margin and the patient is instructed to look upward. Never perform this maneuver in the setting of a potentially ruptured globe.

The depth of the anterior chamber can be assessed. When the anterior chamber is shallow the iris is bowed forward over the lens. Under these conditions, the nasal iris is seen in shadow when the light is directed from the opposite side (Fig. 11). As

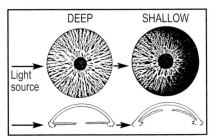

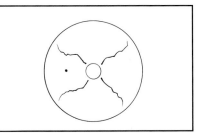

Fig. 11 Estimation of anterior chamber depth

Fig. 12 Examination of the posterior segment includes an assessment of the vessels, macula, and disc as well as the vitreous and peripheral retina.

the shallowness of the anterior chamber increases, so does the shaded view of the nasal iris. A shallow anterior chamber may indicate:

1. a narrow angle that could close with pupillary dilation;
2. angle-closure glaucoma when associated with an elevation of intraocular pressure; or
3. traumatic ocular perforation or laceration.

Posterior Segment

Examination of the posterior segment should include an assessment of the vitreous, disc, vessels, macula, and peripheral retina (Fig. 12). Improved visualization of these structures is best appreciated through a dilated pupil. Dilation of the pupil should not be done in the following circumstances:

1. Do not dilate if assessment of anterior chamber depth suggests a shallow chamber and a narrow angle, because of the risk of precipitating angle-closure glaucoma;
2. Do not dilate if the patient has had a cataract extraction with implantation of an iris-supported intraocular lens. These implant lenses were popular at one time but are no longer used today. The dilation of the iris on these patients could result in a dislocated implant;
3. If the patient is undergoing neurological observation and pupillary signs are being followed (e.g., a head-injured patient), do not dilate until the neurologist or neurosurgeon thinks it is safe to do so.

Vitreous

The vitreous is a jelly-like substance located between the lens and retina. With aging, the vitreous shrinks and often pulls away from its attachments to the retina and disc. Tissue or cells may be displaced, causing the symptom of vitreous floaters, or vitreous movements against the retina may result in the experience of flashing lights.

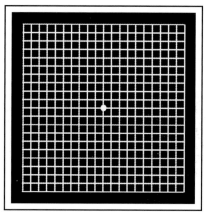

Fig. 13 Amsler grid testing. Shown here is the typical grid pattern of white lines against a black background.

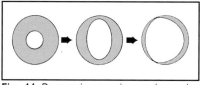

Fig. 14 Progressive cupping or increasing cup-to-disc ratio in the right eye in glaucoma.

Vessels

The retinal blood vessels are normally transparent, and their color is due to the blood. During arteriosclerosis the blood vessel wall becomes visible, progressing from a "copper-wire" appearance to a later "silver-wire" color. Where arterioles meet veins, a common sheath is found; thickening of the arteriole can cause indentation of the vein, or arteriovenous nicking. This can lead to thrombosis and vein occlusion.

Macula

The macula is the region of the retina responsible for central vision and color detection. In the center of the macula is a pit called the fovea which in young patients produces a well-defined reflex. If asymmetry in the foveal reflexes occurs in a patient with a visual disturbance, this suggests a retinal problem.

In addition to ophthalmoscopic examination, the macula can be evaluated by the Amsler grid test (Fig. 13). The test is carried out by having the patient look with one eye at a time at a central spot on a page with horizontal and vertical parallel lines making up a square grid pattern. The patient is asked to note irregularities in the lines. Irregularities may be reported as lines that are wavy, that seem to bow or bend, that are pure gray or fuzzy, or that are absent in certain areas of the grid. With the chart held at a normal reading distance of 30 centimeters from the eye, the Amsler grid measures 10 degrees on each side of fixation. This allows the entire macula to be evaluated.

Optic Disc

The normal optic disc is slightly oval in the vertical meridian and has a pink color due to capillarity. There is a central depression on the surface of the disc called the physiologic cup. The size of the physiologic cup varies among individuals. The pigmented coats of the eye — the retinal pigment epithelium and the choroid — frequently fail to reach the margin of the optic disc, producing a hypopigmented crescent. Such crescents are especially common in myopic eyes on the temporal side of the optic disc. Conversely, an excess of pigment may be seen in some eyes, producing a heavily pigmented margin along the optic disc. The retinal nerve fibers are ordinarily nonmyelinated at the optic disc and retina, but, occasionally, myelination may extend onto the surface of the disc and retina, producing a dense, white, superficial opacification.

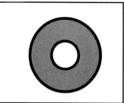

Fig. 15A The normal neural rim is pink

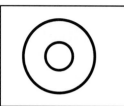

Fig. 15B the neural rim is pale in an old ischemic optic neuropathy.

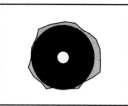

Fig. 16 Hyperemia of the disc and indistinct disc margins may occur in papilledema, optic neuritis, or ischemic optic neuropathy.

The optic disc should be evaluated as follows:

1. *The Cup-to-Disc Ratio.* Most normal patients have a cup-to-disc (C/D) ratio of less than 0.5. A higher C/D ratio or asymmetry between the discs is suggestive of glaucoma. Figure 14 shows progressive cupping in glaucoma.
2. *The Color of the Neural Rim.* A normal neural rim will have a pink color and should be similar in both eyes (Fig. 15A). In an old ischemic optic neuropathy the neural rim will be pale (Fig. 15B).
3. *Contour of the Disc Margins.* The disc margin contour should be distinct. In the acute stages of papilledema, optic neuritis, or ischemic optic neuropathy the disc may appear swollen and the margins indistinct (Fig. 16).

Intraocular Pressure

In an emergency case, the most important reason for checking intraocular pressure is to rule out acute angle closure glaucoma, in which condition the pressure is often greater than 40 mmHg. A pressure over 22 mmHg is generally considered above average and should prompt further investigation. The methods which can be used to check intraocular pressure include tactile tension, Schiotz tonometry, applanation tonometry, air-puff tonometry, and digital tonometry.

Tactile Tension

The pressure of the two eyes can be compared by digital pressure on the globes through closed lids. The eye of a patient with angle closure glaucoma will be firm compared to the opposite eye.

Schiotz Tonometry

Schiotz tonometry is readily available in most emergency departments and doctors' offices, and is the technique of choice for the general practitioner. The patient is supine, a topical anesthetic is instilled in the eyes, and the lids are separated, with care being taken to avoid putting pressure on the globe. The tonometer is used initially with a 5.5-gram weight in place. The tonometer is held as perpendicular as possible and is gently lowered onto the central cornea for a few seconds to determine the scale reading. The less the corneal indentation, the lower the scale reading and the higher the intraocular pressure. If the scale reading is 3 units or less for either eye, the measurement should be repeated. Add weights to the 5.5-gram weight to a total of 7.5, 10.0, or 15.0 grams as necessary to reach the scale reading in the range of 3.5 to 8.0 units. Refer to the calibration scale for Schiotz tonometers to determine the intraocular pressure for a particular plunger load (Appendix D).

Carefully clean the tonometer with an alcohol swab after each use to prevent transmission of disease such as viral conjunctivitis to other patients. The tonometer should not be re-used until it is dry; otherwise a chemical keratoconjunctivitis can be induced.

Applanation Tonometry
The equipment for this test is not as readily available as the Schiotz tonometer. It is a slit-lamp attachment that takes more experience to master, but results in a more accurate measurement.

Air-Puff Tonometer
The air-puff tonometer is an expensive instrument which is not readily available. It does not require use of a topical anesthetic, but is not as accurate as applanation or Schiotz tonometry.

Digital Tonometry
An easy-to-use, expensive portable device (Tono-Pen) that applanates a small surface of the cornea of 1.5 mm. A digital reading is obtained. This device is advantageous when dealing with irregular or scarred corneas. It has become a popular device with ophthalmologists.

Nontraumatic Red Eye

The differential diagnosis of nontraumatic red eye conditions are listed in Appendix E.

Pre-Septal Cellulitis

Pre-septal cellulitis is characterized by erythema and swelling of the eyelids (Plate 2). The infection is confined to the anterior structures of the periorbita.

Predisposing factors include a history of an upper respiratory tract infection, trauma to eyelids, or an external ocular infection. It must be differentiated from an orbital cellulitis, which can result in a permanent loss of vision. In pre-septal cellulitis the patient has normal vision, no proptosis, normal ocular motility, and no pain with eye movements. *Hemophilus influenzae* is the organism most commonly associated with this condition in children under five years of age, and *Staphylococcus aureus* and *Streptococcus sp.* in adults.

Workup
- Cultures are obtained from the nasopharynx, conjunctiva, and blood.
- The patient should be examined by an ophthalmologist to rule out orbital involvement.
- If the patient is unable to cooperate for the examination, or if there is any suspicion of orbital cellulitis, then a computed tomography (CT) scan should be ordered.

Treatment. In mild to moderate cases the prescribed therapy for pre-septal cellulitis is oral antibiotics:
- In adults, e.g., cephalexin hydrochloride (Keflex®) 250 mg q. 6 h. for 10 days.
- In children, e.g., cefaclor (Ceclor®) 40 mg/kg/day (maximum 1 gm/day) q. 8 h. for 10 days.

In severe cases intravenous antibiotics are administered. For example:
- In adults, ceftriaxone 1 to 2 g, IV, q.12 h. and vancomycin 0.5 to 1 g, IV, q 12 h.
- In children, ceftriaxone 100 mg/kg/day in two divided doses and vancomycin 40 mg/kg/day in three to four divided doses.

Chalazion

Chalazion may be manifested initially as diffuse eyelid swelling which results from blockage of the duct of a meibomian gland (Plate 3). Acutely, the obstruction may be secondary to infection by *Staphylococcus sp.* When the infection resolves, a painless nodule may remain which points to the skin or conjunctival side. Recurrent chalazia are often seen in association with blepharitis; appropriate treatment will decrease the incidence of this condition.

Workup. There is effectively no workup for the treatment of this condition.

Treatment
- Warm compresses can be applied for 10 minutes four times a day.
- Topical antibiotic such as ciprofloxacin hydrochloride (Ciloxan®) can be applied q.i.d.

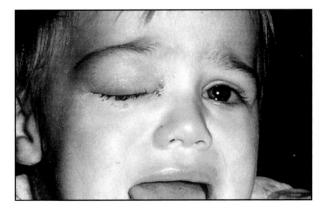

Plate 2
Lid swelling and erythema in a patient with preseptal cellulitis

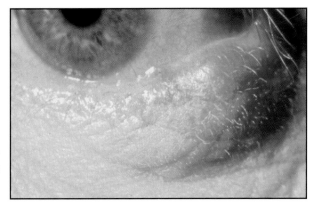

Plate 3
Chalazion characterized by localized lid swelling due to obstruction of a meibomian gland

- If the condition does not resolve in four to six weeks and is of cosmetic concern to the patient, the affected area can be incised and drained under local anesthesia; infants and children usually require general anesthesia. The incision is usually made on the conjunctival side of the tarsal plate, which obviates a skin incision and resultant scar.

Acute Dacryocystitis
Acute dacryocystitis is a blockage of the lacrimal duct which impedes the flow of tears through the lacrimal drainage system. Stasis occurs, which can result in a secondary bacterial infection and swelling and tenderness of the lacrimal sac (Plate 4). The organism most commonly associated with this condition in children under five years of age is *Hemophilus influenzae*, and in adults is *Staphylococcus aureus* (usually penicillinase-resistant).

Workup. Pressure is applied to the lacrimal sac to express material through the puncta, and a conjunctival culture is prepared.

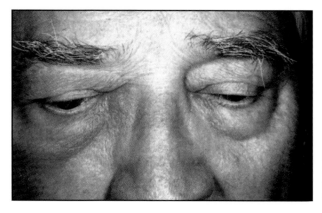

Plate 4
Dacryocystitis with swelling over the lacrimal sac and tearing

Treatment. In mild to moderate cases oral antibiotics are prescribed:
- In adults, Keflex® 250 mg q. 6 h. for 10 days;
- In children, Ceclor® 40 mg/kg (maximum 1 g/day) in divided doses every 8 hours for 10 days.

In severe cases intravenous antibiotics are administered as for pre-septal cellulitis:
- Adults may receive nafcillin 1.5 g and penicillin 3 million units q. 4 h.
- Children may receive ampicillin 200 mg/kg/day and chloramphenicol 11 mg/kg/day. If the organism is sensitive to ampicillin, the chloramphenicol is discontinued.
- When the infection resolves, a dacryocystorhinostomy is recommended to provide a drainage channel for the tears.

Blepharitis

Blepharitis is characterized by debris on the eyelashes, erythema of lid margins, and misdirection or loss of lashes (Plate 5). It may be associated with conjunctivitis, keratitis, or neovascularization of the cornea (Plate 6). Blepharitis may be seborrheic and/or secondary to *Staphylococcus sp.* Rarely, the lids may be infected by pubic lice (pediculosis).

Treatment of Staphylococcal and/or Seborrheic Blepharitis
- Warm compress should be applied b.i.d. to the eyelids to remove scales, and the lid margins cleansed with diluted Johnson's® Baby Shampoo applied with a cotton swab or a specially formulated eyelid cleanser such as Lids & Lashes™.
- Ciloxan® ointment may also be applied to the eyelids at bedtime.
- Artificial tears are used if there is associated keratitis or dry eye, e.g., dextran 70 / hydroxypropyl methylcellulose (Tears Naturale® II), applied q.i.d. and p.r.n. Preservative-free tears are also available without risk of toxicity, e.g., dextran 70 / hydroxypropyl methylcellulose (Bion Tears®).

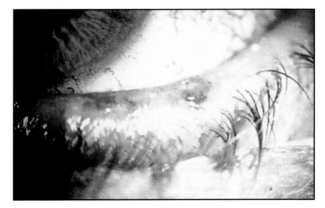

Plate 5
Blepharitis as character-
ized by erythema of the lid
margins and scales on the
lashes

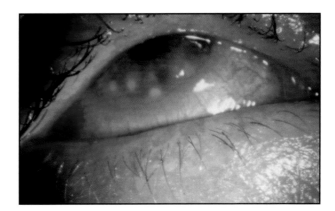

Plate 6
Blepharo-keratitis with
sterile immune infiltration
of the peripheral cornea

- If these measures fail to resolve the problem, then the patient should be referred to an ophthalmologist.
- A short course of a topical steroid/antibiotic combination such as dexamethasone/tobramycin (Tobradex®) may be useful, if there is significant inflammation (Appendix F).
- Tetracycline or doxycycline is useful in refractory cases, especially in those associated with acne rosacea.

Treatment of Pediculosis-Associated Blepharitis. Pubic lice (pediculosis) involvement of the eyelids requires a distinct treatment:
- A 20% fluorescein solution applied to lashes will cause the adult lice to fall off.
- Eggs must be removed manually.
- A 30% incidence of other venereal diseases exists, and this should be ruled out by appropriate testing.

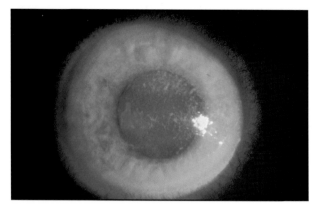

Plate 7
Severe dry eye syndrome with a diffuse punctate keratitis that is best seen with fluorescein dye under cobalt blue light

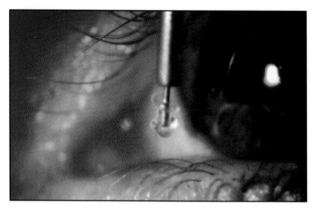

Plate 8
Silicone punctum plug used to enhance the tear film in dry eyes

Dry Eye

Dry eye is a common ocular condition characterized by irritation and burning. Symptoms are often worse when blinking is reduced during activities such as reading, watching TV, and driving. Contact lens tolerance becomes reduced as the contact lenses and eyes become dry. The eyes may have a lackluster appearance, redness, and a decrease in the tear film (Plate 7).

Workup
- Rose Bengal will stain devitalized cells of the cornea and conjunctiva in advanced cases of a dry eye condition.
- Schirmer strips will measure the amount of tear production. The strips are placed in the inferior conjunctival fornix and draped over the lid margin. The amount of wetting is determined after a five minute period. Less than 10 mm of wetting is suggestive of a dry eye.

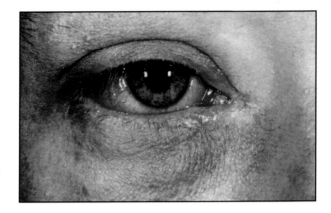

Plate 9
Allergic conjunctivitis with swelling of the lids and conjunctiva

Treatment
- Artificial tears are recommended a few times per day to every hour (e.g., Tears Naturale® II or Bion Tears®).
- Lubricating ointment can be given at bedtime (e.g., Tears Naturale® P.M. — preservative-free ophthalmic ointment)
- Humidifier may be helpful at home and in the workplace.
- Punctal plugs can be inserted to enhance the tear film (Plate 8). This is similar to placing a stopper in a bathtub which will decrease the outflow.

Allergic Conjunctivitis

Itching is the hallmark of allergic conjunctivitis. Other symptoms include tearing, redness, and chemosis (swelling of the conjunctiva). The condition may be unilateral or bilateral (Plate 9). The patient often has a history of atopy (allergic symptoms, rhinitis, asthma, eczema). There may be a history of allergies to dust, pollen, grass, cats, dogs, etc.

Workup
- Conjunctival scraping is optional.
- Giemsa stain may show eosinophils.

Treatment
- Mast cell stabilizers/antihistamine combinations can be prescribed, e.g., olopatadine hydrochloride (Patanol®) b.i.d.
- Cold compresses and topical antihistamines can be applied, e.g., emedastine difumarate (Emadine®) t.i.d.
- Topical nonsteroidals may be effective alone or in combination with the above drugs, e.g., ketorolac (Acular®).
- If highly symptomatic, the patient can be referred to an ophthalmologist.
- A short course of a mild topical steroid could be prescribed, e.g., fluorometholone acetate (Flarex®) q.i.d.

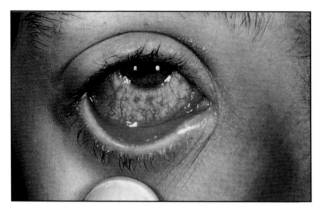

Plate 10
Adenoviral conjunctivitis with lid swelling, conjunctival injection, and tearing

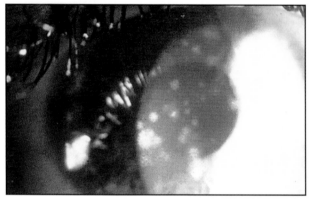

Plate 11
Adenoviral keratoconjunctivitis with subepithelial corneal infiltrates

Adenoviral Conjunctivitis

Adenoviral conjunctivitis is a highly contagious disease (for up to 10 days) characterized by redness, tearing, and a variable degree of photophobia (Plate 10). Follicular hypertrophy of the conjunctiva, which is difficult to detect in the absence of a slit lamp, microscopically represents focal collections of lymphocytes. Keratitis may be absent or limited to superficial punctate keratitis or subepithelial infiltrates (Plate 11). Enlarged pre-auricular lymph nodes may be palpated and their presence is helpful in confirming the diagnosis, as they are never seen in bacterial conjunctivitis except with the gonococcal organism.

Workup. Cultures are unnecessary, since diagnosis is based on clinical evaluation.

Treatment
- No specific antiviral therapy is available.
- Cold compresses can be applied for patient comfort.

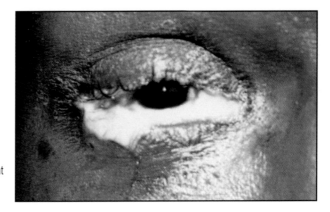

Plate 12
Bacterial conjunctivitis characterized by a purulent discharge that was due to gonorrhea

- Artificial tears (e.g., Tears Naturale® II or Bion Tears® q.i.d and p.r.n.) or astringents (e.g., antazoline phosphate / naphazoline hydrochloride) can be used.
- Prophylactic precautions should be observed by the patient's family members and friends.
- Children should stay away from school for 7 to 10 days.
- If the examiner is uncertain of the diagnosis, it should be assumed that the cause is bacterial, and the condition treated with a topical antibiotic.

Bacterial Conjunctivitis

The symptoms of bacterial conjunctivitis are redness and purulent discharge (Plate 12). There is no pre-auricular node enlargement except in cases of gonococcal conjunctivitis. This condition is less common than viral conjunctivitis.

Workup. In severe cases or those involving a neonate, a Gram stain and culture can be prepared.

Treatment
- Broad-spectrum fluoroquinolone antibiotics (e.g., Ciloxan® q.i.d.) are prescribed.
- In children under five years of age infection may be by *Hemophilus influenzae*. Ciloxan® or tobramycin (Tobrex®) can be used as treatment.
- In cases of gonococcal conjunctivitis, the patient may be given ceftriaxone 1 g in a single dose. If corneal involvement exists, or cannot be excluded because of eyelid swelling and chemosis then the patient should be hospitalized and treated with ceftriaxone 1 g IV q. 12 h. to 24 h. In penicillin-allergic patients consideration can be given to ciprofloxacin 500 mg p.o. single dose. Topical Ciloxan® drops q. 2 h. and or topical bacitracin ointment.

Chlamydia

This is a venereal disease which is usually seen in young sexually active adults. The ocular symptoms of chlamydial infection include redness and mucoid discharge, with or without photophobia. The pre-auricular lymph nodes may be enlarged. Follicular hypertrophy of the conjunctiva is characteristically seen by slit-lamp

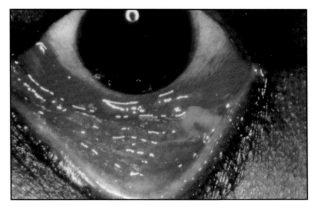

Plate 13
Chlamydial infection characterized by redness, mucoid discharge, and follicular hypertrophy

examination, and later in the disease course a superior micropannus of the cornea may develop (Plate 13). This condition is refractory to topical eye medications, and unlike adenoviral conjunctivitis which usually resolves in less than one month, it may become chronic if not treated.

Workup
- The patient should be referred to an ophthalmologist.
- Clinical diagnosis is made based on the signs and chronicity.
- A Giemsa stain, culture, and fluorescent antibody stain can be performed, but false negatives may occur.

Treatment
- Tetracycline 250-500 mg p.o. q.i.d., doxycycline 100 mg p.o. b.i.d. or erythromycin 250-500 mg p.o. q.i.d. for three weeks; or a single dose of azithromycin 1 g.
- The patient's sexual partner must be similarly treated for the same duration.

Herpes Simplex

Primary Herpes Simplex
The first exposure to herpes simplex virus in 90% of cases results in subclinical, usually mild disease. Resistance increases with age, so that primary infection is exceedingly rare in early adult life. Characteristically, the young child is infected by salivary contamination from an adult who has labial herpes. The incubation period is three to nine days. The clinical features of herpes simplex are both ocular and nonocular.

Ocular disease. Characteristics are vesicular eruption (especially lower lid and medial canthus) (Plate 14), conjunctivitis, regional lymphadenopathy, and occasional corneal epithelial disease. Symptoms are frequently unilateral.

Nonocular Disease. The following forms of the disease may be present:
- Gingivostomatitis — The symptoms are fever, malaise, cervical lymphadenopathy, and sore throat.

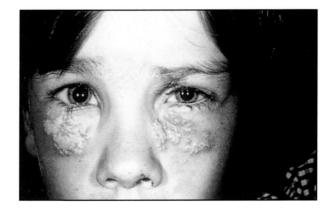

Plate 14
Primary herpes simplex
dermatitis with bilateral
facial involvement

- Pharyngitis — In college students, a primary attack of herpes simplex virus frequently results in a pharyngitis with vesicles on the tonsils.
- Cutaneous disease — Generally, type I occurs above the waist and type II below the waist. This disease may be seen in wrestlers, rugby players, and as a herpetic whitlow in dentists.
- Genital infection — Type II of the infection is more common than type I and is characterized by balanitis in males and cervicitis/vulvovaginitis in females. Patients may exhibit fever, myalgia, extensive vesicular lesions, and inguinal and pelvic lymphadenopathy.

Recurrent Herpes Simplex

The virus develops a "symbiosis" with man, and trigger mechanisms such as trauma, fever, sunlight, emotional stress, steroids, and menses provoke viral shedding, and immunological functions may be overcome. The trigeminal ganglion is a reservoir for the type I disease. The virus has a 50% recurrence rate over five years, and the recurring condition may be highly localized on the lips, nose, chin, eyes (lids, conjunctiva, corneal epithelium, corneal stroma, uvea), and genitals.

Workup. Since this is a clinical diagnosis, cultures are usually unnecessary.

Treatment. The various forms of herpes simplex require specific treatment:
- **Blepharitis** may occur without conjunctival or corneal disease. If it is recurrent, this is consistent with herpes simplex; herpes zoster does not recur. If there is skin but no lid involvement, no topical antiviral treatment is necessary. If the lid margin is involved, then prophylactic antivirals (e.g., Viroptic™ 5x/day) are applied to the conjunctiva.
- **Conjunctivitis** may occur without lid or corneal disease and the patient may have an enlarged pre-auricular lymph node. Ophthalmic referral is recommended and an antiviral (e.g., Viroptic 9x/day) may be applied.
- **Keratitis** occurs in the following forms:

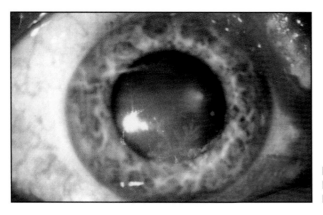

Plate 15
Herpes simplex dendritic
keratitis

(i) **Punctate keratitis** is characterized by raised clusters of opaque epithelial cells, as evidenced with fluorescein stain. Referral to an ophthalmologist is recommended. If diagnosis is unequivocal, a topical antiviral (e.g., Viroptic 9x/day) may be applied. In the case of an equivocal diagnosis, treatment should be deferred and the patient followed closely.

(ii) **Dendritic keratitis** is recognized by desquamation in the center of plaques of swollen epithelial cells (Plate 15). The typical linear branching ulcer (stains with fluorescein) has overhanging margins of swollen opaque cells, which are laden with virus (stains with rose bengal). Ophthalmic referral is recommended and an antiviral (e.g., Viroptic 9x/day) should be applied.

(iii) **Geographic keratitis** results from progression of dendritic keratitis; a geographic epithelial defect (stains with fluorescein) is lined by heaped-up opaque cells (stains with rose bengal) and may be associated with steroid use in dendritic keratitis. Ophthalmic referral is recommended and an antiviral (e.g., Viroptic 9x/day) should be applied.

(iv) **Stromal keratitis** is an immunologic disease characterized by corneal stromal infiltrates and/or edema. Corneal inflammation that may be associated with iritis and keratic precipitates results from antibodies directed at viral antigens. Ophthalmic referral is recommended. If the epithelium is intact, a topical steroid, such as fluorometholone acetate (Flarex®) 5x/day and an antiviral cover (e.g., Viroptic 5x/day) may be applied. If the stromal keratitis is associated with an epithelial disease, an antiviral (e.g., Viroptic 9x/day) should be applied until the epithelium heals (approximately 14 days), after which a topical steroid can be added.

Herpes Zoster
Herpes zoster tends to occur in children under 14 and in adults over 40 years of age. Its incidence is five times greater in those over 80 years of age than in adults between 20 and 40. A 50% incidence of being HIV positive has been found in male patients between the ages of 20 and 40 in New York City. The development of herpes zoster may be the first manifestation of AIDS.

The varicella virus which causes chickenpox can lie dormant in the sensory ganglia and later reactivate as shingles or herpes zoster (Plate 16). Causes of reactivation are unknown but may be related to aging, immune compromise (e.g., AIDS, lymphoproliferative diseases, systemic steroids), and trauma to the involved ganglion. Although chickenpox is contagious, it should not cause herpes zoster; however, children and adults who have not had chickenpox can contract the disease from herpes zoster patients. Once the virus is reactivated, it may be contained (zoster sine herpete), or spread to the brain, skin, eye, or enter the bloodstream. The virus has a predilection for dermatome T3-L3, but the most common site is the trigeminal nerve. Cutaneous lesions of herpes zoster are histopathologically identical to varicella, but have a greater inflammatory reaction which can cause scarring.

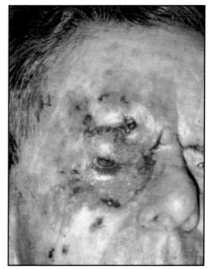

Plate 16
Herpes zoster ophthalmicus with trigeminal nerve distribution

The dermatome pattern of herpes zoster may occur in three sites supplied by branches of the trigeminal nerve:

- The ophthalmic nerve distribution (V1) where it occurs 20 times more frequently than at the V2 or V3 sites. Frontal involvement is the most common, including the upper lid, forehead, and superior conjunctiva, which are supplied by supraorbital and supratrochlear branches (Fig. 17). Alternatively, it may spread to the lacrimal and nasociliary area which supplies the cornea, iris, ciliary body, and the tip of the nose;
- The maxillary nerve distribution (V2);
- The mandibular nerve distribution (V3).

The virus may affect none, any, or all of these branches. Involvement of the nasociliary nerve often leads to infection of the eye. Hutchinson's rule (1860s) states that ocular involvement is frequent, if the side of the tip of the nose is involved.

Clinically, herpes zoster is characterized by a prodrome, skin disease, and ocular complications. The patients may experience pain, burning, itching, hyperesthesia in the dermatome area, followed by erythema, macules, papules, and vesicles which become confluent and may form deeply pitted scars (dermis affected by necrotic process). Ocular complications include lid scarring and exposure, muscle palsies, conjunctivitis, episcleritis, scleritis, keratitis, uveitis, and retinitis.

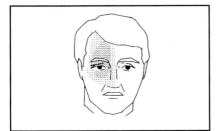

Fig. 17 Herpes zoster ophthalmicus is characterized by vesicular skin eruptions in the distribution of any of the branches of the trigeminal nerve.

Workup. Systemic evaluation for underlying malignancy is not indicated since the yield is low.

Treatment
- Compresses can be applied to the affected areas of the skin.
- Medication for pain relief can be given.
- Antivirals may be prescribed: acyclovir 800 mg p.o. five times a day or famciclovir 500 mg t.i.d. for seven days may prevent serious ocular disease and may accelerate resolution of skin lesions. It is more effective if initiated within 72 hours of the onset of the disease. Topical antiviral therapy is ineffective for ocular treatment.
- The patient should be referred to an ophthalmologist to rule out ocular involvement.
- Topical steroids (e.g., Flarex q.i.d.) will improve comfort and decrease the chance of corneal scarring when there is corneal stromal inflammation.
- Lubrication with preservative-free artificial tears (e.g., Bion Tears®) q. 1 – 2 h. may be helpful.
- Cycloplegic agents (e.g., Cyclogyl® 2% b.i.d.) will relieve ciliary spasm in corneal and anterior chamber inflammation making the patient more comfortable and dilating the pupil to prevent posterior synechiae (iris-lens adhesions).
- Pain may be severe during the first two weeks and analgesics (e.g., acetaminophen with or without codeine) may be required. An antidepressant (e.g., amitriptyline 25 mg p.o. t.i.d.) may be beneficial as depression frequently develops during the acute phase of HZV infection. Antidepressants also may help post-herpetic neuralgia. Management of post-herpetic neuralgia should involve the patient's primary medical doctor.

Toxic Conjunctivitis

This condition may be secondary to a topical medication (e.g., antibiotics, glaucoma drops, etc.), from a consumer product such as eye make-up or moisturizing creams, or from *molluscum contagiosum*. The patient will often complain of irritation and redness. If the cause is secondary to *molluscum contagiosum* the focal lesions may be seen on the face and/or lids (Plate 17 A & B).

Workup. No workup is required.

Treatment
- If drug-induced, it is important to discontinue the topical medications. If the patient has a history of glaucoma then alternative medications need to be prescribed.

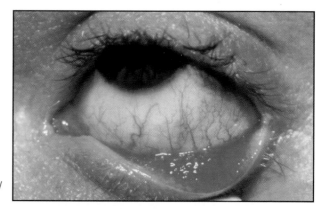

Plate 17A
Toxic conjunctivitis secondary to *molluscum contagiosum*

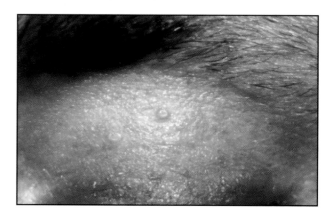

Plate 17B
Molluscum lesions of the upper lid

- If the patient is not taking any topical medications, then consideration should be given to the potential irritative effects from a consumer product. Discontinuing eye make-up and creams may be effective in resolving the symptoms.
- If the diagnosis is *molluscum contagiosum* then the small skin lesions can either be excised or curetted.

Recurrent Corneal Erosions

Patients with recurrent corneal erosions experience pain, photophobia, and redness, but have no acute history of trauma. Corneal erosion, which stains with fluorescein, is due to the lack of strong corneal epithelial attachments. The erosion frequently occurs on awakening, since the corneal epithelium becomes more edematous during eyelid closure and more susceptible to focal sloughing. Predisposing factors for this condition may be an old traumatic injury (e.g., fingernail, tree branch, paper), corneal dystrophy, and bullous keratopathy (i.e., corneal edema).

Workup. No workup is required.

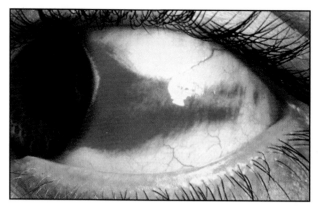

Plate 18
Subconjunctival hemorrhage as evidenced by a bright red color

Treatment
- Antibiotic ointment or drops (e.g., Ciloxan®) and a cycloplegic agent (e.g., Cyclogyl® 1%) should be prescribed.
- A pressure patch should be applied.
- Ophthalmic referral is recommended.
- Hypertonic drops and/or ointment, e.g., sodium chloride 5% drops during the day and ointment at bedtime to be used over a period of weeks to months to dehydrate the epithelium and decrease the risk of erosions.
- A bandage soft contact lens can be used for a period of weeks to months to decrease the chance of epithelial erosions.
- Anterior stromal puncture can be performed if the patient continues to develop erosions in the same location. A 25-gauge needle can be used to make multiple punctures into the anterior stroma in the area of the erosion. This allows for the development of stronger adhesions and decreases the risk of erosions. However, the technique is contra-indicated in erosions that occur close to the pupillary axis.
- In patients who continue to have recurrent corneal erosions, the excimer laser can be used to perform a phototherapeutic keratectomy. After the epithelium is mechanically removed, five to ten microns of stromal tissue are vaporized. This allows for greater epithelial adherence to the somewhat roughened surface and causes essentially no change in refractive error.

Subconjunctival Hemorrhage
A ruptured vessel with blood accumulation in the subconjunctival space describes a subconjunctival hemorrhage (Plate 18). It is often accompanied by a history of coughing, vomiting or straining. The patient may be taking warfarin sodium (Coumadin®) or aspirin.

Workup
- If the patient's history is negative for Valsalva's maneuver, a blood pressure reading should be taken.

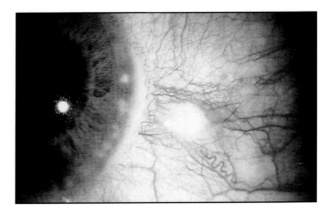

Plate 19
Phlyctenule of the conjunctiva with an elevated white nodule surrounded by conjunctival injection

- The patient on Coumadin should undergo tests to ensure that the rate of blood clotting is in the desired range.
- In the case of recurrent subconjunctival hemorrhage, a complete blood count should be taken to rule out a blood dyscrasia.

Treatment. Reassuring the patient is all that is necessary since the hemorrhage will resolve spontaneously.

Phlyctenule

A phlyctenule is a small, pinkish-white nodule in the center of a hyperemic area of conjunctiva (Plate 19). Although it is seen most frequently near the limbus, it may occur anywhere on the bulbar conjunctiva. Less commonly, it involves the cornea where it is associated with vascular ingrowth. The patient's history should be used to rule out the possibility of any foreign body. Phlyctenules may be caused by a hypersensitivity reaction to an antigenic stimulus such as *Staphylococcus aureus* or the tubercle bacilli.

Workup
- The patient should be referred to an ophthalmologist.
- A tuberculin skin test and chest X ray is recommended if the patient is in a high-risk group.

Treatment
- A topical steroid (e.g., Flarex q.i.d.) may be prescribed.
- Any associated staphylococcal blepharitis should be treated.

Episcleritis

Episcleritis is characterized by a salmon-pink hue of the superficial layer of the eye, with involvement of the conjunctiva and episclera (Plate 20). At least one-third of the lesions are tender to touch. Simple episcleritis may be sectoral in 70% or generalized in 30% of patients. In nodular episcleritis, unlike in nodular scleritis, the nodules which form are moveable with a cotton swab.

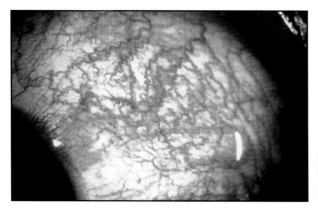

Plate 20
Episcleritis with sectorial injection of the conjunctiva and episcleral tissue

Workup. Ophthalmic referral is recommended.

Treatment. A topical steroid (e.g., Flarex® q.i.d.) will cause resolution of the inflammation.

Scleritis
Scleritis is frequently bilateral and, characteristically, associated with pain. The ocular surface has a purplish hue with involvement of the deep episcleral vessels (Plate 21). Systemic diseases, such as collagen vascular, ulcerative colitis, Crohn's, and sarcoidosis, are present in 50% of patients. The eight-year mortality rate is 30%, with death usually due to a vascular disease. Scleritis may be classified as simple (in its most benign form), nodular (the nodule is immobile when pushed with a cotton swab), or necrotizing (the majority of these patients have rheumatoid arthritis).

Workup
- Ophthalmic referral is recommended.
- The patient should be evaluated for an underlying systemic disease.

Treatment
- A topical steroid (e.g., Flarex®) may be prescribed to reduce the inflammation.
- A systemic nonsteroidal anti-inflammatory medication is recommended, e.g., indomethacin (Indocid®) 25 mg p.o. t.i.d.
- If there is no significant improvement, then systemic steroids can be prescribed with a tapering dose.

Corneal Ulcers
Patients with corneal ulcers may experience redness, pain, photophobia, and tearing. The cornea will have a whitish infiltrate with an overlying epithelial defect that will stain with fluorescein (Plate 22). Hypopyon (layered pus in the anterior chamber) may be associated with a corneal ulcer. Patients most at risk are those who

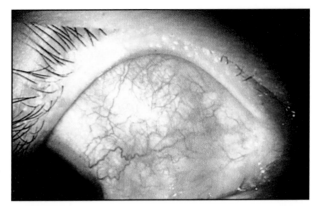

Plate 21
Scleritis with diffuse involvement of the deep episcleral vessels

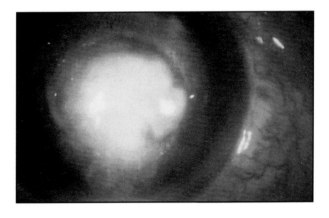

Plate 22
Corneal ulcer with central white infiltrate and a hypopyon

wear contact lenses, those with blepharitis and dry eyes, or those who have experienced corneal trauma. The most common causes are bacterial infections, e.g., by *Pseudomonas*, *Staphylococcus aureus*, or *Streptococcus pneumoniae*. Less common organisms include fungi and *Acanthamoeba*. Infection with the latter is relatively rare and is seen predominantly in contact lens wearers. Risk factors for acquiring *Acanthamoeba* include swimming with contact lenses and rinsing lenses with tap water or home-made saline.

Workup
- Ophthalmic referral is recommended.
- The cornea should be scraped for Gram stain and culture if the infiltrate is in the visual axis, is greater than 2 mm, or is progressive despite antibiotic treatment.

Treatment
- Ciloxan® alone or in combination with Tobrex® may be used for the majority of corneal ulcers

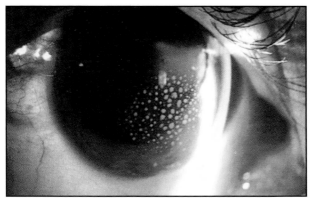

Plate 23
Iritis with granulomatous (mutton-fat) keratic precipitates

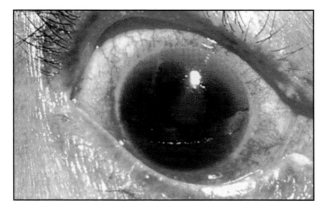

Plate 24
Acute angle closure glaucoma with a ciliary injection, swollen cornea, and marked elevation in intraocular pressure

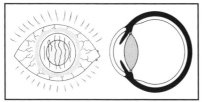

Fig. 18 Acute angle closure glaucoma is manifested by elevated intraocular pressure, and is associated with redness, ciliary injection, corneal edema, a nonreactive mid-dilated pupil, and a relatively narrow anterior chamber angle.

- Topical fortified antibiotics, e.g., tobramycin (15 mg/mL) and cefazolin (50 mg/mL) should be considered for advanced corneal ulcers (> 2 mm)
- If a fungal infection is noted with a Gram stain or culture, then topical natamycin and miconazole can be started.
- If *Acanthamoeba* is detected, then the patient can be placed on propamidine isethionate 0.1% (Brolene®) drops and ointment, polyhexamethyl biguanide (PHMB), and oral ketoconazole.

Iritis

Iritis is characterized by redness, photophobia, tearing, and decreased vision. A ciliary flush is prominent and the pupil is constricted secondary to the inflammation (Plate 23). Slit-lamp examination shows an anterior chamber reaction manifested

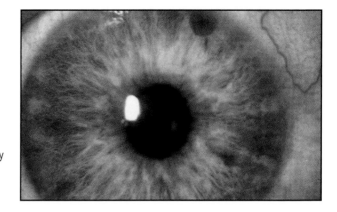

Plate 25
Laser peripheral iridotomy noted superiorly in a patient who had angle-closure glaucoma

by inflammatory cells, flare (protein leakage), and keratic precipitates. Testing with fluorescein stain should be done to rule out corneal abrasion and a herpes simplex dendrite.

Workup
- Ophthalmic referral is recommended.
- If condition is persistent or recurrent, underlying systemic disorders (e.g., ankylosing spondylitis, sarcoidosis) should be ruled out.

Treatment. A topical steroid (e.g., Flarex® q.1-2 h.) and a cycloplegic agent (e.g., Cyclogyl® 1% or homatropine 5% q. 6 h.) should be prescribed. A NSAID (e.g., Acular®) may be used if there is a contraindication to steroid drops; for example, a history of steroid-induced glaucoma.

Acute Angle Closure Glaucoma
Acute angle closure glaucoma is characterized by redness, severe pain, photophobia, and decreased vision (Fig. 18, Plate 24); the patient may also experience nausea and vomiting. Elevated intraocular pressure, corneal edema, and a nonreactive mid-dilated pupil may also be present. This tends to occur more frequently in the hyperopic (farsighted) eye due to a relatively narrow anterior chamber.

Workup
- Tonometry should be performed to confirm diagnosis.
- Ophthalmic referral is recommended.

Treatment
- Effective medications include: pilocarpine 2% q. 5 min. x4, then q.1 h., betaxolol hydrochloride (Betoptic® S) drops q.12 h., isosorbide 1-2 gm/kg p.o. x1, acetazolamide (Diamox®) 250 mg p.o. q. 6 h. or 500 mg IV, and mannitol IV 20% 1-2 gm/kg.
- Laser iridotomy should be performed in the affected eye and a prophylactic iridotomy in the contralateral eye (Plate 25).

Traumatic Red Eye

Corneal Abrasions
The patient with a corneal abrasion has a history of trauma caused, for example, by a tree branch, fingernail, or contact lens. The patient will complain of pain, photophobia, redness, and blurred vision.

Workup. The diagnosis is confirmed by demonstrating an epithelial defect with fluorescein dye under cobalt blue light (Plate 26).

Treatment
- Antibiotic drops or ointment (e.g., Ciloxan®) should be instilled along with a cycloplegic agent (e.g., Cyclogyl® 1% or homatropine 5%).
- A pressure patch should be applied.
- Analgesic medication may make the patient more comfortable.
- Topical anesthetics should never be prescribed as an analgesic, as this will inhibit corneal epithelial healing.
- Patient follow-up is recommended on a daily basis to determine epithelial healing and ensure the absence of an infection.

N.B.: Contact lens related abrasions should not be patched, as a subclinical infection may be present. Instead, these abrasions should be treated with antibiotic drops active against *Pseudomonas* (e.g., Ciloxan q. 2 h.).

Contact Lenses
Contact lens wearers may develop a red eye due to a variety of pathophysiologic causes: mechanical, hypoxic, immunologic, chemical toxicity, and infection. The most important concern is the possibility of the development of an infected ulcer that can lead to corneal scarring and a permanent decrease in vision (Plate 27).

Workup. Refer to Appendix G for the differential diagnosis of red eye in contact lens wearers.

Treatment
- All patients with a red eye should remove their contact lenses.
- Referral to an ophthalmologist is necessary to determine the cause of red eye.

Ultraviolet Keratitis
Ultraviolet keratitis is usually bilateral and is characterized by redness, photophobia, tearing, and blepharospasm (Plate 28). Usually the patient has been welding or using a sun lamp without proper eye protection. Typically, the symptoms appear 6 to 10 hours after exposure. The pain is usually out of proportion to the clinical findings.

Workup. Fluorescein staining will reveal the presence of superficial punctate keratitis.

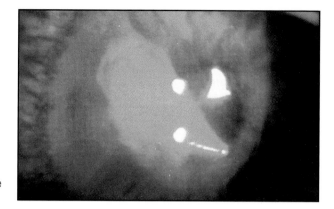

Plate 26
Corneal abrasion stains
green with fluorescein dye
under cobalt blue light

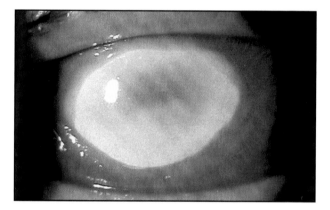

Plate 27
Acanthamoeba corneal
ulcer secondary to contact
lens wear

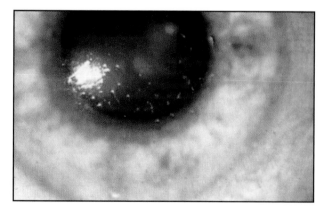

Plate 28
Ultraviolet light burn to the
eye with evidence of an
epithelial punctate keratitis

Treatment
- An antibiotic drop or ointment (e.g., Ciloxan®) should be instilled along with a cycloplegic agent (e.g., Cyclogyl® 1%).
- The more severely affected eye should be patched, and the patient instructed to apply a patch to the less affected eye at home.
- A pain medication can be prescribed.
- Follow-up is recommended to ensure epithelial healing.

Chemical Injuries

Alkali injuries are often more severe than acid injuries due to the fact that acids tend to coagulate tissue and inhibit further penetration into the cornea. Clinical findings of chemical injury vary with severity of the injury: a mild injury is characterized by conjunctivitis, superficial punctate keratitis, and an epithelial defect of the cornea and conjunctiva (Plate 29); a severe injury exhibits blanching of limbal blood vessels and opacification of the cornea (Plate 30).

Alkali Agents
- Ammonia — Commonly found in household ammonia (7% cleaning agent), fertilizer, and refrigerant (strongest concentration is 29%). Penetration of the eye occurs in less than a minute, which makes the injury difficult to treat by irrigation.
- Lye (sodium hydroxide) — Commonly found in drain cleaners (e.g., Draino), it ranks second to ammonia in severity of injury induced.
- Hydroxides — Common forms are potassium hydroxide (found in caustic potash) and magnesium hydroxide (found in sparklers and flares). The chemical burns are similar to those caused by sodium hydroxide.
- Lime ($CaOH_2$=calcium hydroxide) — This is one of the most common substances involved in ocular burns and is found in plaster, cement, mortar, and whitewash. However, because it reacts with the epithelial cell membrane to form calcium soaps which precipitate, it penetrates the eye poorly.

Acid Agents
- Sulfuric Acid (H_2SO_4) — Commonly found in batteries and industrial chemicals, injuries are often due to battery explosions with resultant lacerations, contusions, and foreign bodies. When H_2SO_4 comes into contact with the water in the corneal tissue, heat is released charring the tissue and causing severe injury.
- Sulfur Dioxide (SO_2) — Commonly found combined with oils in fruit and vegetable preservatives, bleach, and refrigerants. It forms sulfurous acid (H_2SO_3) when it combines with water in corneal tissue. Injury is caused by the H_2SO_3 rather than the freezing effect of SO_2; it denatures proteins, inactivates numerous enzymes, and penetrates tissue well because of its high lipid and water solubility.
- Hydrofluoric Acid (HF) — Commonly used for etching and polishing glass or silicone, frosted glass, refined uranium and beryllium, alkylation of high octane gasoline, production of elemental fluoride, inorganic fluorides, and organic fluorocarbons. Much of the damage to the eye is caused by the fluoride ion.

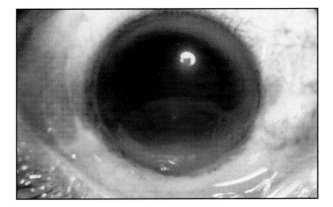

Plate 29
Mild chemical injury with fluorescein staining of the inferior cornea and conjunctiva

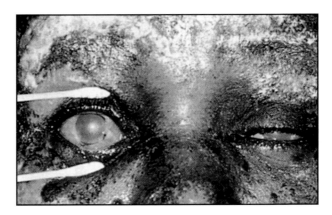

Plate 30
Severe chemical injury to the eyes that resulted in corneal opacification

- Other Acids — These include chromic acid, hydrochloric acid, nitric acid, and acetic acid.

Workup. Since this emergency situation requires immediate treatment, no workup is recommended.

Treatment. The emergency physician should initiate the following procedures:
- Initial vision testing is deferred for chemical injuries until the irrigation and pH testing has been completed.
- Topical anesthetic drops are instilled to facilitate irrigation.
- The eye should be irrigated with a nontoxic liquid (water, ionic solutions, buffered solutions), but acidic solutions are not recommended as they are too risky. An IV drip for at least 30 minutes is recommended with the eyelids retracted. The pH can be checked using litmus paper, applied to the conjunctival surface to assess the adequacy of irrigation in achieving a neutral pH.

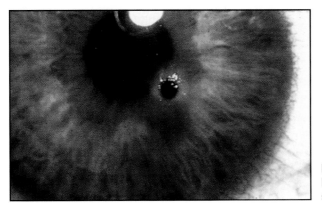

Plate 31
Metallic foreign body of the superficial cornea

- Any particulate matter should be removed from the fornices. A moistened cotton-tip applicator can be used to remove chemical matter.
- A cycloplegic agent (e.g., Cyclogyl® or homatropine) will prevent posterior synechiae and alleviates ciliary spasm.
- An antibiotic drop or ointment can be applied, along with a pressure patch.

The ophthalmologist may initiate the following treatment:
- The patient should be followed closely to ensure the healing of the epithelium.
- The intraocular pressure should be lowered, if it is elevated (e.g., prescribe Betoptic® S and/or Diamox®).
- Topical steroids may be used to decrease inflammation but should be limited to no more than two weeks in the case of a persistent epithelial defect. Prolonged steroid use in the presence of an epithelial defect can cause the cornea to melt.
- Bandage contact lenses may be used, if the epithelium is not healed by patching.
- If the cornea heals with scarring and vascularization, the prognosis for restoring vision using a corneal transplant is poor because of the high incidence of graft rejection and failure.

Corneal Foreign Bodies
A corneal foreign body may be present in the patient exhibiting redness, foreign-body sensation, photophobia, and a history of trauma (Plate 31).

Workup. Rule out full thickness corneal penetration that if present should prompt urgent ophthalmic referral.

Treatment
- A topical anesthetic should be instilled and the foreign body removed with a needle (e.g., 22-gauge) or a burr drill if done under slit-lamp magnification. If the foreign body cannot be seen, the upper lid should be everted to examine the lid margin and the palpebral conjunctival surface (Plate 32).

Traumatic Red Eye **43**

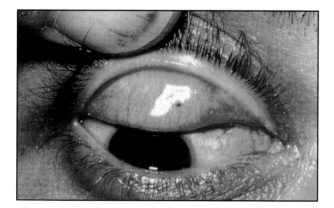

Plate 32
Superficial keratitis of the
cornea secondary to a
retained foreign body
beneath the upper lid

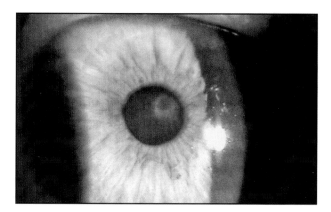

Plate 33
Central corneal scar
following foreign body
removal

- It is best to remove all the associated rust, but not essential. It tends to diffuse out of the cornea with time.
- Be extremely gentle when removing foreign bodies overlying the pupil as excessive manipulation can lead to corneal scarring and a decrease in vision (Plate 33).
- A cycloplegic agent (e.g., Cyclogyl® 1%) should be instilled, along with an antibiotic drop or ointment (e.g., Ciloxan®).
- A pressure patch should be applied.
- Follow-up is recommended to determine epithelial healing, and to ensure the absence of infection or residual rust.

Intraocular Foreign Bodies
A small foreign body travelling at a high speed can penetrate the eye without the patient's awareness. The symptoms are highly variable, depending on the site of

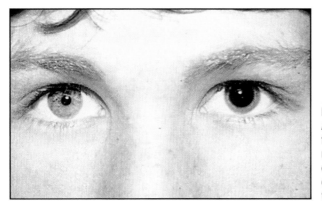

Plate 34
A retained intraocular foreign body that has resulted in siderosis with discoloration of the iris, dilated pupil, and retinal toxicity

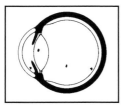

Fig. 19 Intraocular foreign bodies can be found in a variety of sites: in the anterior chamber, lens, vitreous, or retina.

penetration and intraocular structures affected. All foreign bodies made of iron should be removed, since they can cause significant intraocular damage (siderosis bulbi) (Plate 34). However, glass, aluminum, gold, and silver are inert and usually cause little or no chronic intraocular damage (Fig. 19).

Workup
- An X ray (Waters' view and lateral) should be ordered if an intraocular foreign body is suspected.
- Ophthalmic referral is recommended.
- If the foreign body cannot be visualized on examination, a CT scan should be ordered to determine whether the foreign body is intraocular or extraocular.

Treatment. To extract an intraocular foreign body, magnetic extraction or vitrectomy with foreign body instrumentation is usually indicated. Most foreign bodies outside of the eye in the orbit can usually be left without adverse sequelae.

Blow-Out Fracture
A blow to the periorbital structures can cause a fracture of the orbital floor and result in periorbital ecchymosis, infraorbital nerve anesthesia, and limitation of upgaze (Plate 35). There are two theories as to the mechanism of a blow-out fracture: (1) That a blow to the orbit causes a sudden increase in intraorbital pressure which results in the fracture, and (2) A blow to the inferior orbital rim results in a buckling of the orbital floor.

Other fractures to the orbit are less common. A medial fracture of the thin ethmoidal bone may be associated with subcutaneous emphysema of the eyelids. A fracture at or near the optic canal through which the optic nerve and ophthalmic artery pass may cause damage to the optic nerve, resulting in visual loss.

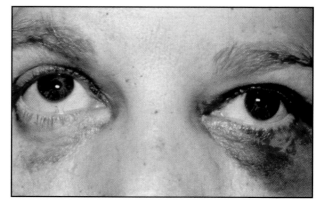

Plate 35
Blow-out fracture to the left orbital floor with periorbital ecchymosis and limitation of upgaze

Workup
- An X ray (Waters' view and lateral) and a CT scan (anteroposterior and coronal views of orbits) should be taken.
- Ophthalmic referral is recommended.
- The eye should be checked for any associated intraocular damage (e.g., hyphema, scleral rupture, traumatic cataract, macular edema, choroidal rupture, retinal tears, or retinal detachment).

Treatment
- Patients should try to refrain from nose-blowing and coughing.
- Systemic antibiotics should be prescribed (e.g., Keflex® 250 mg p.o. q.i.d. x 10 days).
- Surgical repair of the orbital fracture is dependent on the CT scan findings and/or clinical signs during the subsequent one to two weeks.
- Surgery is indicated in cases of soft tissue entrapment associated with diplopia, enophthalmos greater than 2 mm, or fractures involving more than one-half of the orbital floor.

Hyphema

Hyphema is caused by blunt or penetrating trauma and is characterized by decreased vision, ciliary injection, and a view of the fundus which is hazy due to the presence of blood (Fig. 20, Plate 36). A ruptured globe must be ruled out. Children often have an unreliable history, and it is important to rule out any intraocular foreign body. A tear in the ciliary body or iris usually occurs in the area of the angle. The incidence of rebleeds is 20% to 25%, usually between the third and fifth days.

Workup. No workup is recommended.

Treatment
- Ophthalmic referral is recommended.

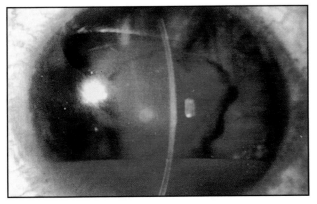

Plate 36
Traumatic hyphema with layering of blood inferiorly and a clot covering the pupil

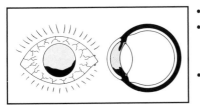

Fig. 20 Usually the result of blunt trauma, hyphema (or blood in the anterior chamber) is characterized by decreased vision, ciliary injection, and a hazy view of the fundus due to the presence of blood.

- A protective eye shield should be applied.
- Confined either to bedrest with bathroom privileges or to limited activity. No strenuous activity allowed.
- A cycloplegic agent and antiglaucoma medication should be prescribed. No aspirin-containing products should be given.
- Aminocaproic acid (Amicar®) reduces the incidence of secondary hemorrhage and may be taken orally by the patient.
- Patients should be told that they are at an increased risk for the development of glaucoma secondary to damage to the angle, as well as for retinal detachment. Patients therefore should be followed on a regular basis for the rest of their lives.

Blunt Trauma Injury

Hyphema, cataract, iridodialysis (Plate 37), scleral rupture (Plate 38), traumatic mydriasis, choroidal rupture, optic neuropathy, retinal tears and/or retinal detachment may be present in blunt trauma injuries. Retinal hemorrhages in children older than one month is a strong indicator of the shaken baby syndrome (Plate 39).

Workup. No workup is required.

Treatment
- Ophthalmic referral is recommended.
- A protective eye shield should be applied.
- Cataracts, scleral ruptures, retinal tears, and/or retinal detachments should be surgically managed.

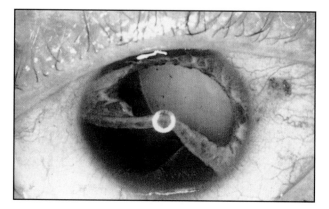

Plate 37
Traumatic iridodialysis and cataract

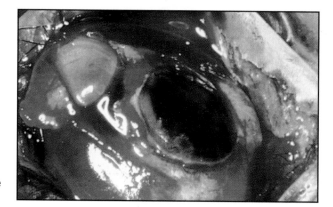

Plate 38
Severe blunt trauma that resulted in a scleral rupture with extrusion of the lens

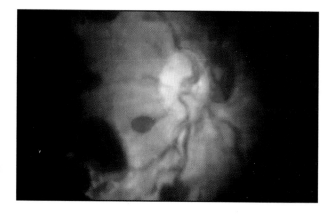

Plate 39
Scattered retinal hemorrhages secondary to head trauma in a case of child abuse

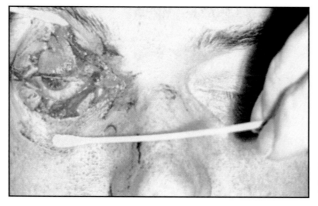

Plate 40
A severe injury to the lids
from a dog bite

- Any associated hyphema should be treated as previously described.
- Any case of suspected child abuse should be reported to the appropriate authorities.

Lacerations and Perforations

Most ocular injuries present with obvious redness and pain. However, some injuries provide few warning signs. For example, a sharp perforation may produce minimal redness and escape attention. In all cases of perforating lid injuries the possibility of an ocular perforation should be considered (Plate 40). Failure to recognize a perforating eye injury and to initiate antibiotic therapy may result in loss of the eye from endophthalmitis, a severe infection within the globe.

Workup. No workup is required.

Treatment
- Ophthalmic referral is recommended.
- A protective eye shield should be applied.
- Tetanus toxoid injection is given if updating required.

The following are the treatment options depending on the affected site:
(i) Lid — if the lid margin is involved, a suturing technique is critical to prevent notching.
(ii) Tear Drainage System — repair includes re-approximation of the severed canaliculi ends with internal stents to prevent chronic tearing.
(iii) Conjunctiva — if an isolated injury, repair is usually unnecessary.
(iv) Sclera — always suspect a puncture or laceration when the conjunctiva is involved; scleral laceration requires sutures and treatment with IV antibiotics to prevent endophthalmitis.
(v) Cornea — full-thickness lacerations require sutures, and puncture wounds that leak can be glued with tissue adhesives.
(vi) Lens — cataract extraction is indicated for this injury.
(vii) Vitreous — a vitrectomy may be required.

Decreased Vision in a White Eye

The emergency physician should be able to make the diagnosis of a sudden decrease in vision. Early treatment of central retinal artery occlusion and ischemic neuropathy secondary to giant cell arteritis can be sight-saving.

Vein Occlusion

The presence of scattered superficial retinal hemorrhages may indicate a central retinal vein occlusion (CRVO) or a branch retinal vein occlusion (BRVO) (Fig. 21, Plates 41, 42). In CRVO the hemorrhages are located primarily at the posterior pole but may be seen throughout the fundus; in BRVO the hemorrhages are located in the distribution of the occluded vein. Vein occlusions are often encountered in older patients with hypertension and arteriosclerotic vascular disease. Carotid occlusion may produce a similar fundus picture. In rare cases, diseases that alter blood viscosity, such as polycythemia vera, sickle-cell disease, and leukemia induce retinal vein occlusions.

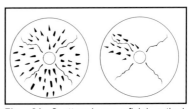

Fig. 21 Scattered superficial retinal hemorrhages are indicative of central retinal vein occlusion (left) or branch retinal vein occlusion (right).

The acute hemorrhages and disc swelling resolve with time; however they may be followed by the development of shunt vessels from the choroidal circulation to the retina and ocular neovascularization.

Workup
- Ophthalmic referral is recommended.
- The intraocular pressure in both eyes should be taken, since patients with vein occlusions have a higher incidence of glaucoma.
- Fluorescein angiography may be performed to determine the extent of retinal ischemia and/or macular edema. In this special technique, intravenous injection of fluorescein dye will help demonstrate the integrity of the retinal and choroidal vasculature.

Treatment
- In CRVO, panretinal laser photocoagulation is indicated, if the retina shows significant ischemic change. This technique prevents the neovascularization of the anterior chamber angle which can lead to glaucoma.
- In BRVO, focal laser photocoagulation may improve visual acuity and may be indicated for chronic macular edema. If neovascularization of the retina develops, then focal laser photocoagulation may resolve the neovascular tufts and prevent a vitreous hemorrhage.

Artery Occlusion

Both central retinal artery occlusions (CRAO) and branch retinal artery occlusions (BRAO) are characterized by ischemic whitening of the retina (Plates 43, 44).

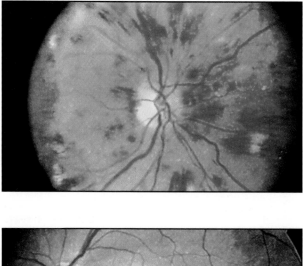

Plate 41
Central vein occlusion with
scattered hemorrhages
and cotton-wool spots

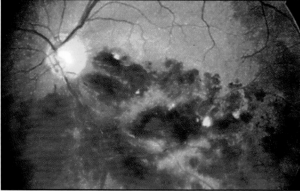

Plate 42
Branch vein occlusion with
scattered hemorrhages
throughout the inferior
retina

Permanent visual loss may be preceded by periods of transient monocular visual loss called amaurosis fugax. The report of a period of visual loss in one eye lasting for several minutes should prompt an investigation of the ipsilateral carotid circulation to seek the presence of an atheroma, which may be the source of emboli that transiently interrupt blood flow to the retina. These patients should be referred to an ophthalmologist, neurologist, or vascular surgeon. In CRAO the fovea appears as a cherry-red spot, since the choroidal vasculature is easily visible through this relatively thinned retinal area (Fig. 22). Central visual acuity may rarely be normal in CRAO, if the blood supply from the choroidal vasculature to the fovea is maintained by a small retinal artery (cilioretinal artery). Most occlusions are caused by emboli that may be seen on the disc in CRAO or in an artery in BRAO. A chronic cherry-red spot is also a feature of metabolic storage diseases such as Tay-Sachs disease and a variant of Niemann-Pick disease in which the ganglion cells become swollen as a result of the deposition of metabolic substances.

The disc, which is supplied by other branches of the ophthalmic artery, does not swell unless the occlusion is in the ophthalmic or carotid artery, proximal to the

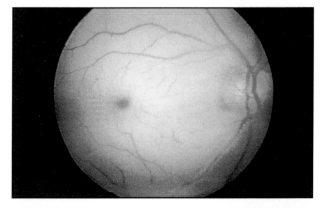

Plate 43
Central retinal artery occlusion as characterized by a cherry-red spot on the fovea

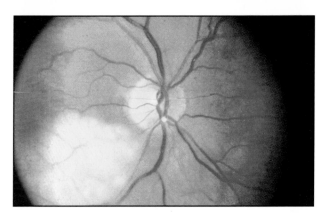

Plate 44
Branch retinal artery occlusion as characterized by an embolus on the disc and ischemic whitening of the inferotemporal retina

origin of the central retinal artery. The characteristics of the eye's vascular supply explain the preservation of some vision in the presence of a complete CRAO. If part of the retina derives its blood supply from the choroidal circulation via a cilioretinal artery, its function is spared. Since cilioretinal arteries are relatively common anomalies, present in up to 25% of eyes, small islands of vision may be preserved after CRAO. If the territory of the cilioretinal artery includes both the macula and the disc, a visual acuity

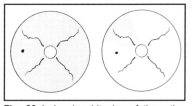

Fig. 22 Ischemic whitening of the retina is indicative of a central retinal artery occlusion (left) or a branch retinal artery occlusion (right).

of 20/20 is possible but there is severe loss of peripheral field. After a CRAO the retinal edema slowly resolves, and the death of the ganglion cells and their axons leads to optic atrophy. Months later, the characteristic ophthalmoscopic appearance is a pale disc and a blind eye.

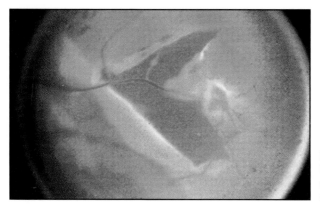

Plate 45
Large retinal tear with
an associated retinal
detachment

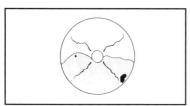

Fig. 23 In retinal detachment the retina appears white when elevated. If the macula is detached, the central vision will be diminished.

Workup
- The patient's history should be taken to determine whether cerebral transient ischemic attacks have occurred.
- The carotid arteries and the heart should be evaluated to determine the source of the emboli.

Treatment
- Less than four hours by history is a true emergency.
- Breathe carbogen (CO_2/O_2 mixture) for vasodilation of retinal arterioles.
- The patient should be given an ocular massage, along with Betoptic® S drops, Diamox® 500 mg p.o., and mannitol 20% 200 mL IV
- Ophthalmic referral is recommended.
- An anterior chamber paracentesis may be performed.

Retinal Detachment
When a retinal tear develops, fluid may accumulate beneath the retina creating a retinal detachment (Plate 45). Typically, the patient with a retinal detachment complains of flashing lights followed by a large number of floaters and then a shade over the vision in one eye. A detachment that is extensive enough to reduce visual acuity usually produces a relative afferent pupillary defect in the involved eye. A visual field deficit is present and the retina appears white when elevated (Fig. 23). There is an increased risk of retinal detachment in patients with myopia, aphakia, pseudophakia, or previous ocular trauma.

Workup. No workup is required.

Treatment
- Ophthalmic referral is recommended.

- Surgical correction is required.
- If the patient's central vision is diminished (i.e., the macula is detached), there appears to be no difference in final visual acuity whether the surgery is performed immediately or after two or three days.

Maculopathy

A sudden decrease in vision often associated with metamorphopsia (wavy vision) suggests a macular problem. The macula may be affected acutely by edema, hemorrhage, and/or exudates. Unless the macular disease is extensive, a relative afferent pupillary defect may not be present. Differential diagnosis includes diabetes mellitus (Plate 46), histoplasmosis, central serous retinopathy, and macular degeneration.

In age-related macular degeneration, the visual changes may be secondary to drusen, to degenerative changes in the retinal pigment epithelium, and to subretinal neovascular membranes (new blood vessels) (Plate 47). Drusen are hyaline nodules deposited in Bruch's membrane, which separates the inner choroidal vessels from the retinal pigment epithelium. Drusen may be small and discreet or larger with irregular shapes and indistinct edges. Patients with drusen alone tend to have normal or near-normal visual acuity with minimal metamorphopsia. Degenerative changes in the retinal pigment epithelium may occur with or without drusen. These degenerative changes are manifested as clumps of hyperpigmentation and/or depigmented atrophic areas. The effects on visual acuity vary.

Workup
- Ophthalmic referral is recommended.
- Fluorescein angiography may be performed to determine the source of macular leakage.

Treatment
- If leaking vessels and/or microaneurysms are identified in diabetic patients, laser photocoagulation can be performed.
- In the case of choroidal neovascularization in macular degeneration or histoplasmosis, laser photocoagulation can be applied if the vessels are not directly beneath the fovea otherwise photodynamic therapy is the preferred option.
- In central serous retinopathy, a fluorescein angiogram will often identify a focal leakage point of the retinal pigment epithelium which causes an accumulation of fluid beneath the retina. The majority of cases resolve spontaneously. However, the course can be shortened by using a laser to seal the defect in the pigment epithelium.

Vitreous Hemorrhage

Vitreous hemorrhage is characterized by a hazy view of the fundus with a reduced or altered red reflex (Plate 48). The most common causes are posterior vitreous detachment, proliferative diabetic retinopathy, vein occlusion with neovascularization of the retina, retinal tear without detachment, retinal detachment, macroaneurysm of the retina, and trauma. Treat as suspected ruptured globe if vitreous hemorrhage occurs in setting of trauma.

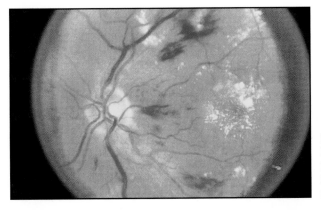

Plate 46
Background diabetic retinopathy as characterized by scattered retinal hemorrhages and exudates

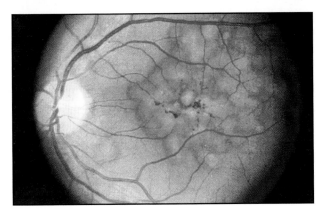

Plate 47
Macular drusen and pigment changes as seen in age-related macular degeneration

Workup
- Ophthalmic referral is recommended.
- A B-scan ultrasound should be performed to rule out an associated retinal detachment and/or mass lesion such as a malignant melanoma.

Treatment
- The majority of hemorrhages will resolve spontaneously in a few weeks to months.
- Vitrectomy may be indicated in nonclearing vitreous hemorrhages. It may also be combined with laser photocoagulation if there is an associated retinal tear or neovascularization, or a scleral buckle if there is a retinal detachment.

Optic Neuritis
Optic neuritis is usually seen in patients between 20 and 50 years of age, who typically complain of a decrease in vision and pain with eye movement. Patients usually have decreased color vision. The optic disc is swollen (Plate 49, Appendix H) or it may appear normal in retrobulbar optic neuritis (Fig. 24). Of these patients, over 50% will develop multiple sclerosis.

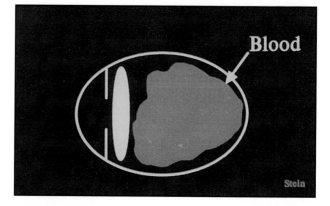

Plate 48
Diagram showing a vitreous hemorrhage that obscures visibility of the fundus

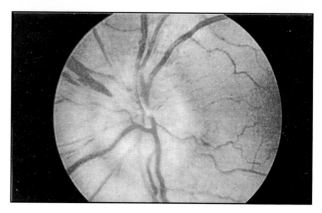

Plate 49
Swollen optic disc in optic neuritis. Papilledema has a similar appearance except this condition is bilateral and visual acuity is usually unaffected.

Workup
- Ophthalmic referral is recommended.
- The visual field should be checked and a follow-up test performed to determine the course of visual loss.
- Brain MRI should be performed to rule out demyelination.

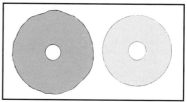

Fig. 24 Optic neuritis is characterized by a swollen optic disc and indistinct disc margins (left) or a normal appearing disc in retrobulbar optic neuritis (right).

Treatment
- No specific ocular therapy is generally indicated.
- Controlled studies of systemic steroids have failed to demonstrate any difference in long-term visual outcome between treated and untreated groups.
- If the brain MRI is positive for demyelinating disease, then intravenous steroids (methylprednisolone) should be administered. This has been shown to decrease the rate of development of multiple sclerosis.

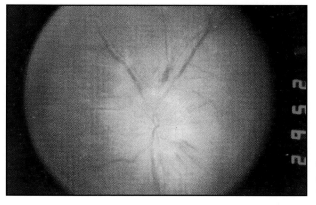

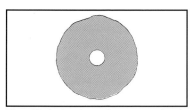

Fig. 25 Ischemic optic neuropathy is
accompanied by a pale swelling of the optic
disc and indistinct disc margins.

Ischemic Optic Neuropathy

Ischemic optic neuropathy is usually seen in patients over 50 years of age and is characterized by a sudden decrease in vision and a swollen optic disc (Fig. 25, Plate 50). The disease process is idiopathic in the majority of cases. Occasionally the condition is secondary to giant cell arteritis (GCA). This is an inflammatory condition of medium to large arteries with a predilection for extradural cranial arteries including the ophthalmic vessels. The symptoms and signs of GCA are headache, jaw claudication, and temporal artery tenderness, but it is important to note that patients with GCA may exhibit only visual symptoms.

Workup
- The erythrocyte sedimentation rate (ESR) should be obtained to rule out GCA. In this condition the ESR is usually elevated.
- Temporal artery biopsy is the definitive test to confirm the diagnosis. Biopsy of the temporal artery may demonstrate the findings of giant cells, fragmentation of the elastica with surrounding chronic inflammation and occlusion of the vessel.

Treatment
- No specific treatment exists for idiopathic ischemic optic neuropathy.
- Ophthalmic referral is recommended.
- If GCA is suspected, systemic steroids should be started immediately to protect the patient from bilateral visual loss.
- Systemic steroids do not compromise biopsy results and may protect fellow eye while awaiting confirmation of diagnosis by biopsy.
- Steroids are usually tapered and maintained for a minimum of 9 to 12 months.

Cortical Blindness

Patients with cortical blindness present with acute loss of vision in both eyes, resulting from a stroke to the occipital or visual cortex of the brain. Because the pathways serving the pupillary light reflex are separate from those carrying visual information, the patient with cortical blindness has normal pupillary reactions. This finding along with a normal ophthalmoscopic examination helps establish the diagnosis. Some patients with cortical blindness show some improvement; others expire due to severe neurological damage.

Workup
- CT scan of the brain.
- Neurologic referral.
- Ophthalmic referral to document extent of visual loss.

Treatment. No specific treatment is available.

Diplopia

In evaluating a patient who complains of double vision, it is important to determine whether this occurs on a monocular basis or with binocular vision and that disappears when one eye is occluded. Monocular diplopia is not a neurologic dysfunction but may be secondary to a corneal anomaly (e.g., epithelial irregularity from a corneal dystrophy, referred to as anterior basement membrane dystrophy) or from a problem of the lens (e.g., cataract). True neurologic diplopia means that two separate, equally bright images are visualized with one of the images disappearing when one eye is closed. Neurologic causes of diplopia include a 3rd, 4th, or 6th nerve palsy.

Third Nerve Palsy

The third nerve (oculomotor nerve) innervates four eye muscles: the superior rectus, the medial rectus, the inferior rectus, and the inferior oblique. It carries the parasympathetic fibers to the sphincter of the iris, and innervates the levator muscle of the upper lid.

In third nerve palsy there may be diplopia, ptosis, and/or a dilated pupil (Plate 51). The eye is deviated out and down. The etiology of this condition is as follows: aneurysm 20%, vascular disease (diabetes, hypertension, athero-sclerosis) 20%, tumors 15%, trauma 15%, and miscellaneous and undetermined 30%.

Workup
- If the pupil is fixed and dilated, other causes should be ruled out (e.g., Adie's pupil, or contamination with a dilating drop).
- If the pupillary dilatation is secondary to third nerve palsy, this constitutes a medical emergency and prompt neurosurgical referral is required. Cerebral angiography and CT scan should be ordered to rule out an intracranial aneurysm or neoplasm. If the pupil is not involved, diabetes, hypertension, collagen vascular disease, and GCA (if the patient is more than 55 years of age) should be ruled out.

Treatment
- Ophthalmic referral is recommended.
- The eye can be patched to alleviate diplopia.
- The majority of third nerve palsies not involving the pupil resolve within six months.
- If muscle weakness persists for more than 12 months, then surgery can be performed to improve cosmesis.

Fourth Nerve Palsy

The fourth nerve (trochlear nerve) supplies the superior oblique muscle which moves the eye downward and inward. The palsy causes elevation of the eye with resultant vertical diplopia and involves a torsional component making images appear tilted. Congenital fourth nerve palsies may initially be asymptomatic and a head tilt (towards the opposite shoulder to minimize the diplopia) may be the only

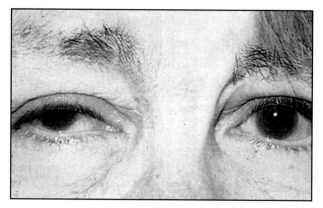

Plate 51
Third nerve palsy characterized by ptosis, dilated pupil, and deviation of the eye laterally

symptom; as image fusion ability diminishes over time, diplopia results. Acquired fourth nerve palsies are usually secondary to head trauma.

Workup
- If the fourth nerve palsy is isolated, it is not necessary to test for any underlying systemic diseases.

Treatment
- Ophthalmic referral is recommended.
- Prismatic correction in eyeglasses or surgical intervention may be indicated, depending on the severity and the duration of the palsy.

Sixth Nerve Palsy
The sixth nerve (abducens nerve) innervates the lateral rectus muscle which moves the eye out. The palsy is characterized by horizontal diplopia (images side-by-side), most prominent in the field of gaze of the underactive lateral rectus muscle. The patient may be partially or completely unable to move the eye laterally (Plate 52).

Workup
- Obtain a patient history; children often have a history of a recent viral illness or immunization.
- In adults, diabetes, hypertension, collagen vascular disease, and GCA (if over the age of 55) should be ruled out.
- If sixth nerve palsy is not isolated (i.e., associated with other nerve palsies) or if the patient has papilledema, then a CT scan is indicated to rule out a neoplastic process.

Treatment
- Ophthalmic referral is recommended.

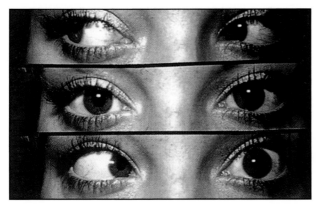

Plate 52
Sixth nerve palsy of the left eye characterized by limited motility on gaze to the left side (lower sequence)

- Isolated sixth nerve palsies usually resolve spontaneously within six months.
- An eye patch can be placed over the affected eye, or if the patient wears eyeglasses, tape can be placed over the lateral portion of the lens.
- If muscle weakness persists for more than 12 months, then surgery can align the eyes in primary gaze.

Myasthenia Gravis

Myasthenia gravis is an autoimmune condition that interferes with neuromuscular transmission in skeletal muscles. Although it can affect any muscle, ptosis and/or double vision are the presenting signs in approximately 50% of patients. Myasthenia gravis may mimic any other ocular motility disorder including 3rd, 4th and 6th nerve disease. A history of intermittent diplopia or ptosis that is worse later in the day is suggestive of myasthenia gravis.

Workup
- Neurologic referral is suggested.
- Ophthalmic referral is recommended.
- Patients with unexplained diplopia and/or ptosis should have an edrophonium chloride (Tensilon) test to rule out myasthenia gravis.

Treatment
- Systemic medication for myasthenia gravis to be initiated by an internist.

Appendixes

Appendix A Ocular complications of systemic diseases	
Disease	**Possible Ocular Findings**
Diabetes mellitus	Background retinopathy: retinal hemorrhages, exudates & microaneurysms.
	Preproliferative retinopathy: cotton-wool spots, intraretinal microvascular abnormalities.
	Proliferative retinopathy: neovascularization, preretinal hemorrhage, vitreous hemorrhage, retinal detachment.
Graves' disease	Lid retraction, exposure keratopathy, chemosis and injection, restriction of eye movements, proptosis, compressive optic neuropathy.
Hypertension	Sclerosis of vessels in longstanding disease; narrowing of vessels, retinal hemorrhages, and/or exudates in severe hypertension.
Rheumatoid arthritis & other collagen vascular diseases	Dry eye, episcleritis, scleritis, peripheral corneal ulceration and/or melting.
Cancer	Metastatic disease to choroid may result in retinal detachment; disease in the orbit can result in proptosis and restriction of eye movements. (e.g., breast, lung cancer)
Sarcoidosis	Dry eye, conjunctival granulomas, iritis, retinitis.
AIDS	Kaposi's sarcoma, cotton-wool spots of retina, cytomegalovirus retinitis.

Appendix B Life-threatening ocular signs	
Findings	**Clinical Significance**
White pupil	In an infant retinoblastoma must be ruled out.
Aniridia (iris appears absent)	May be autosomal dominant (2/3s) or sporadic inheritance. In sporadic cases where the short arm of chromosome 11 is deleted, there is a 90% risk of developing Wilms' tumor; the risk in other sporadic cases is approximately 20%.
Thickened corneal nerves (slit lamp)	Part of the multiple endocrine neoplasia syndrome type IIB. Must rule out medullary carcinoma of the thyroid, pheochromocytoma, and parathyroid adenomas.
Retinal angioma	May be part of the Von Hippel-Lindau syndrome. Autosomal dominant inheritance with variable penetrance. Must rule out hemangioblastomas of the central nervous system, renal cell carcinoma, and pheochromocytoma.
Multiple pigmented patches of fundus	Lesions represent patches of congenital hypertrophy of the retinal pigment epithelium. May be part of Gardner's syndrome characterized by multiple premalignant intestinal polyps together with benign soft tissue tumors (lipomas, fibromas, sebaceous cysts) and osteomas of the skull and jaw. A complete gastrointestinal investigation is indicated. If a diagnosis of Gardner's syndrome is made, prophylactic colectomy is indicated because of the potential for malignant degeneration of colonic polyps.
Third nerve palsy with a dilated pupil	Must rule out an intracranial aneurysm or neoplastic lesion. CT scan should be performed on an emergency basis.
Papilledema	Must rule out an intracranial mass lesion. CT scan should be performed on an emergency basis.
Pigmentary degeneration of the defect retina and motility disturbance	May represent the Kearns-Sayre syndrome. Must rule out a cardiac conduction disturbance with an annual electrocardiogram. May develop an intraventricular conduction defect, bundle block, bifascicular disease, or complete heart block. Patient must be prepared for the possible need to implant a pacemaker.

Appendix C Ocular complications of systemic medications	
Medication	**Ocular Complications**
Amiodarone	Superficial whorl-like keratopathy
Chlorpromazine	Anterior subcapsular cataracts
Corticosteroids	Posterior subcapsular cataracts, glaucoma
Digitalis	Blurred vision, disturbed color vision
Ethambutol	Optic neuropathy
Indomethacin	Superficial keratopathy
Isoniazid	Optic neuropathy
Nalidixic acid	Papilledema
Hydroxychloroquine	Superficial keratopathy and bull's-eye maculopathy
Tetracycline	Papilledema
Thioridazine	Pigmentary degeneration of the retina
Vitamin A	Papilledema

Appendix D	Calibration scale for Schiotz tonometers			
	Plunger Load (gm)			
	5.5	7.5	10.0	15.0
Scale Reading (scale units)	**Intraocular Pressure (mm Hg)**			
0	41	59	82	127
0.5	38	51	75	118
1.0	35	50	70	109
1.5	32	46	64	101
2.0	29	42	59	94
2.5	27	39	55	88
3.0	24	36	51	82
3.5	22	33	47	76
4.0	21	30	43	71
4.5	19	28	40	66
5.0	17	26	37	62
5.5	16	24	34	58
6.0	15	22	32	54
6.5	13	20	29	50
7.0	12	19	27	46
7.5	11	17	25	43
8.0	10	16	23	40
8.5	9	14	21	38
9.0	9	13	20	35
9.5	8	12	18	32
10.0	7	11	16	30
10.5	6	10	15	27
11.0	6	9	14	25
11.5	5	8	13	23
12.0		8	11	21
12.5		7	10	20
13.0		6	10	18
13.5		6	9	17
14.0		5	8	15
14.5			7	14
15.0			6	13
15.5			6	11
16.0			5	10
16.5				9
17.0				8
17.5				8
18.0				7

Appendix E

1. Differential diagnosis of nontraumatic red eye

Feature	Condition		
	Acute Conjunctivitis	**Acute Iritis**	**Acute Glaucoma**
Symptoms	Redness, tearing +/- discharge	Redness, pain, photophobia	Redness, severe pain, nausea, vomiting
Appearance	Conjunctival injection	Ciliary injection	Diffuse injection
Vision	Normal, can be blurred secondary	Moderate reduction halo vision	Marked reduction, to discharge
Cornea	Clear	May see keratic precipitates	Hazy secondary to edema
Pupil	Normal	Small, sluggish to light	Semidilated nonreactive
Secretions	Tearing to purulent	Tearing	Tearing
Test & Comments	Smears may show etiology: bacterial infection = polycytes, bacteria; viral infection = monocytes; allergy = eosinophils	Slit lamp will show cells and flare in the anterior chamber	Elevated intraocular pressure
Treatment	Antibiotic	Steroids Cycloplegics	Pilocarpine Betoptic® S Diamox® Mannitol Laser surgery

2. Differential diagnosis of viral, bacterial, and allergic conjunctivitis

Feature	**Viral**	**Bacterial**	**Allergy**
Discharge	Watery	Purulent	Watery
Itching	Minimal	Minimal	Marked
Pre-auricular lymph node	Common	Absent	Absent
Stain & smear	Monocytes Lymphocytes	Bacteria Polycytes	Eosinophils

Appendix F Ocular complications of topical corticosteroids

Topical corticosteroids alone or in combination with antibiotics should not be administered to the eye by a primary-care physician. They can be helpful when used under the close supervision of an ophthalmologist.

Topical corticosteroids have three potentially serious ocular side effects:

1. **Keratitis**. Herpes simplex keratitis and fungal keratitis are both markedly potentiated by corticosteroids. These agents may mask symptoms of inflammation making the patient feel better while the cornea may be melting or even perforating.

2. **Cataracts**. Prolonged use of corticosteroids, either locally or systemically, will often lead to cataract formation.

3. **Elevated intraocular pressure**. Local application of corticosteroids may cause an elevation of intraocular pressure. Optic nerve damage and loss of vision can occur. The combination of a corticosteroid and an antibiotic carries the same risk.

Appendix G Differential diagnosis of red eye in contact lens wearers

Diagnosis	Findings	Mechanism	Treatment
Corneal abrasion	Epithelial defect Stains with fluorescein	Mechanical Hypoxia	Antibiotic drops (e.g., Ciloxan®)
Superficial punctate keratitis	Punctate corneal staining	Mechanical Chemical toxicity	Artificial tears (e.g., Bion Tears®)
Giant papillary conjunctivitis	Papillary reaction of superior tarsal conjunctiva	Immunologic Mechanical	Mast cell stabilizer (e.g., Patanol®)
Sterile infiltrates	Corneal infiltrate Epithelium usually intact	Immunologic	Antibiotic drops (assume infected)
Infected ulcer	Corneal infiltrate with ulceration Stains with fluorescein	*Pseudomonas, Staphylococcus aureus, etc.*)	Corneal scraping Gram stain and culture. Fortified antibiotic drops, Ciloxan®

Appendix H Differential diagnosis of swollen optic disc

	Optic Neuritis	Optic Neuropathy	Papilledema
Age	< 50 years	> 50 years	Any age
Visual acuity	Decreased	Decreased	Normal
Other symptoms	Pain, especially with eye movement	May have symptoms of giant cell arteritis, headache, jaw claudication, and scalp tenderness	May have associated neurological signs if there is a lesion, e.g., nerve palsy, weakness, or sensory loss in limbs
Disc appearance	Swollen occasionally Normal in retrobulbar optic neuritis.	Swollen	Swollen
Workup	Visual field — if atypical or if no improvement in follow-up a CT scan to rule out mass lesion	Stat ESR. If elevated perform temporal artery biopsy to confirm diagnosis.	Stat CT scan to rule out intracranial mass lesion
Treatment	None	If elevated ESR use systemic steroids. If temporal artery biopsy negative discontinue steroids.	Neurosurgical consult to consider surgery

Appendix I Chronic conditions that may present with acute symptoms

Condition	Symptoms	Comment
Cataract	Decreased vision	Usually a slowly progressive decrease in vision. Occasionally a rapid deterioration in vision especially with posterior subcapsular cataracts that encroach on the visual axis. Cataract types named after anatomical location: cortical, nuclear, anterior and posterior subcapsular. Cataract surgery for visual improvement.
Corneal edema	Decreased vision Photophobia Tearing	May develop following cataract surgery (pseudophakic bullous keratopathy or aphakic bullous keratopathy), or with a corneal dystrophy. Corneal transplant surgery can restore vision.
Macular degeneration	Decreased vision Metamorphopsia	Usually a slowly progressive condition. If rapid decrease in vision or metamorphopsia (wavy vision), possible hemorrhage or exudation in macula. Fluorescein angiogram to determine leakage points. Laser photocoagulation may be of benefit.

Appendix J	Postoperative ocular complications		
Surgery	**Symptoms**	**Possible Diagnosis**	**Ophthalmic Referral**
Cataract	Redness, pain, decreased vision in the first week after surgery	Endophthalmitis (infection within the eye)	Stat
	Foreign body sensation, discharge	Loose suture	Urgent
	Diminished vision months after surgery	Opacified posterior capsule	Non-urgent
		Retinal detachment	Urgent
Corneal transplant	Redness, pain, decreased vision in the first week after surgery	Endophthalmitis (infection within the eye)	Stat
	Foreign body sensation, discharge	Loose suture	Urgent
	Decreased vision months after surgery	Graft rejection	Urgent
Retinal detachment (scleral buckle)	Decreased vision	Recurrent retinal detachment	Urgent
		Vitreous hemorrhage	Urgent
Photorefractive keratectomy (PRK)	Pain in first 48 hours	UV radiation effect & corneal abrasion	Urgent
		Corneal ulcer	Stat
Laser assisted in situ keratomileusis	Pain and decreased vision	Displaced corneal flap or interstitial keratitis	Stat
Blepharoplasty	Lid hemorrhage, pain, diminished vision	Periorbital/orbital hemorrhage	Stat
		Compression of optic nerve	Stat
Dacryocystorhinostomy	Periorbital hemorrhage	Bleeding into soft tissues	Stat

Note: Stat referral = seen within hours; Urgent referral = seen within 24 hours; Non-urgent referral = seen within a few days